The Economic
Transformation
of Eastern Europe

THE ECONOMIC TRANSFORMATION OF EASTERN EUROPE

Views from Within

Edited by BERNARD S. KATZ and LIBBY RITTENBERG

PRAEGER

Westport, Connecticut
London

Library of Congress Cataloging-in-Publication Data

The Economic transformation of eastern Europe : views from within /
   edited by Bernard S. Katz and Libby Rittenberg.
       p.   cm.
   Includes bibliographical references and indexes.
   ISBN 0–275–93825–5 (alk. paper)
   1. Europe, Eastern—Economic policy—1989–   —Case studies.
   2. Europe, Eastern—Economic conditions—1989–   —Case studies.
   3. Privatization—Europe, Eastern—Case studies.   4. Post-communism
   —Europe, Eastern—Case studies.   I. Katz, Bernard S., 1932– .
   II. Rittenberg, Libby.
   HC244.E2447   1992
   338.947—dc20   92–943

British Library Cataloguing in Publication Data is available.

Library of Congress Catalog Card Number: 92–943
ISBN: 0–275–93825–5

First published in 1992

Praeger Publishers, 88 Post Road West, Westport, CT 06881
An imprint of Greenwood Publishing Group, Inc.

Printed in the United States of America

The paper used in this book complies with the
Permanent Paper Standard issued by the National
Information Standards Organization (Z39.48–1984).

10 9 8 7 6 5 4 3 2 1

To the consumers of Eastern Europe

Contents

Figures and Tables

FIGURES

TABLES

Introduction and Overview

The unexpected and dramatic political events since 1989 in Eastern Europe (defined traditionally as Albania, Bulgaria, Czechoslovakia, the German Democratic Republic, Hungary, Poland, Romania, and Yugoslavia) have led to unprecedented calls for economic reform. To a greater or lesser degree, all of these nations are currently seeking the means to bring their economies from a system of state ownership and central planning based on the Soviet model (Yugoslavia deviated the most from the Soviet model when it chose a labor-managed approach), to one characterized by private ownership and market solutions, based on the model of the Western industrialized nations.

The path toward this type of systemic change is an uncharted one. Not only does the process involve shifting production decisions in order to respond to consumer demand as determined by the market through prices, but also it must unburden the public sector by shifting the means of production to private hands. It also includes the creation of institutions and policy-making bodies that will allow private agents to operate efficiently and effectively. All of this must preserve the social fabric of the countries, many of which are threatened by rising ethnic tensions and sub-nationalisms. This volume describes the evolving transformations and the burdens they impose on the economic system.

The pace of change varies among the countries. The path of the former German Democratic Republic, now eastern Germany, will not be discussed here because it is a special case. The three other countries that seem most committed to the process of transformation, as reflected in their actions and political choices, are Czechoslovakia, Hungary, and Poland. Although attention here is focused on them, the study of their successes and failures will surely serve as a guide to the other countries of Eastern Europe, as well as to Third World nations that are also contemplating such change. A chapter on Yugoslavia is also included to consider some of the special problems it faces as it tries to move away from its somewhat unique labor-managed status. However, given the unsettled status of the country itself, it has not been able to articulate a coherent and enforceable policy of change.

The book is divided into three main sections that divide the transformation process into three critical areas: the issue of the transfer of property rights (i.e., privatization issues); problems of economic reform at the macroeconomic level; and microeconomic or firm-level responses to the transformation process. In most cases, the chapters include both a critical analysis of the issue being considered and a brief economic history of the country under examination, as well as comparisons among countries in their past and current policies and generalizations to other countries in the process of or considering change.

This volume differs from many such others insofar as its authors are all academics residing within the country they discuss. Thus, the tone of the chapters tends to be more intimate as authors discuss both previous reform attempts and the current, more structural changes. In reading each chapter, one can often sense the frustration or cynicism as the authors criticize a policy as being too fast or too slow, too marginal or too all-encompassing. Such first-hand impressions, we hope, will aid the reader in understanding the complexity of the transformations underway.

The first four chapters focus on the transfer of ownership or property rights. Jiri Hlavacek makes the general case, using Czechoslovakia as an example, that efficiency cannot be achieved until and unless firms become private entities, even if the major step of price liberalization has been taken. He argues that without private ownership, firms expect paternalistic state behavior and they are more likely to receive subsidies if they exaggerate their production costs (i.e., if they continue to behave inefficiently). Thus, until privatization occurs, the economy will continue to exhibit the undesirable characteristics of a centrally planned one, even if planning per se has ended. Czechoslovakia, he states, is placing more emphasis on privatization than on price liberalization, even though the former is more difficult to achieve. He believes, however, that such a path engenders a superior final outcome, as it creates an economic climate more geared toward profit maximization, and thus efficiency, than does the reverse path.

Zoltan Bara traces the evolution of property rights in Hungary over the post-World War II period, the changes in which have been arguably more extensive than in any other eastern bloc country. He argues that the failure of early reform attempts at the beginning of Hungary's New Economic Mechanism (NEM) can be attributed to the lack of clearly defined property rights and the network of informal relations that persisted. He describes Hungary's unique creation of so-called spontaneous privatization, which began in the 1980s. Despite critics who question its fairness, as former managers often become owners without due compensation to the state, Bara maintains that this method of privatization, along with more traditional ones (such as direct sales to domestic residents and foreigners), promotes the main goal—the establishment of a market economy based on privatization.

Maciej Iwanek reviews the structure of property rights that existed in Poland prior to the 1989 revolution and the new structure that is currently taking shape. He describes the pros and cons of various privatization strategies in terms that can be readily applied to the other countries of Eastern Europe that are undergoing transformation and then provides details on the Polish experience to date. In so doing, the reader recognizes the complexity of the negotiations involved and the extent to which compromises must be made by all parties if the transformation is to be successful. He concludes that because the processes under way are experimental, monitoring and revising of the laws and procedures are inevitable as problems and threats appear.

Ivan Ribnikar's chapter on privatization in Yugoslavia argues that Yugoslavia's so-called market-planned system did not constitute a third way. Without going into the details of the analysis here, he contends that it survived as long as it did by transferring various costs to the future, primarily through inflation and growing domestic and foreign indebtedness. Thus, he believes, this system must be replaced by a true privately based market system, but the introduction of the new system must be particular to conditions in Yugoslavia. He advocates the fairly drawn-out process of privatization detailed in the chapter, especially with regard to the stock of existing capital as opposed to increases in capital.

Jerzy Skuratowicz opens the section on macroeconomic policies during the transition process. Reminding the reader that the course is uncharted and that Eastern Europe is trying to accomplish in a short period what Western Europe took centuries to achieve, he argues that the traditional stabilization policies employed so swiftly and dramatically in Poland have not necessarily had the desired effects on the economy. For example, he argues that in the industrial sector, the large, inefficient enterprises have been able to survive—despite the high interest rates—by borrowing from each other, whereas enterprises engaged in lighter manufacturing, which could have contributed in the long run to greater overall efficiency, have been squeezed out. In agriculture, he argues that smaller farms have responded by reducing the marketable share of their output, leaving the larger farms free to engage in more monopolistic pricing practices. He further argues that the unemployment problem is only exacerbated by policies that have the effect of releasing labor from both industry and agriculture simultaneously. He concludes that Poland may have adopted policies that can only create what he calls "impoverished growth." Policy should be redesigned, he argues, to take into account these and other inappropriate responses and a more coherent and careful look at the timing, costs, and sequencing of the reforms should be adopted.

Ales Bulir describes the previous macroeconomic environment in Czechoslovakia, the basic features of current macroeconomic policy as the country undergoes transformation, and potential pitfalls of designing future policy. He contends that what is referred to as macroeconomic policy under the central planning system should be more appropriately labelled microeconomic policy because government interference was always aimed toward particular firms, regions, or products and their most basic decisions. Bulir defines macroeconomic policy as policy that affects the rules of the economic game through manipulation of basic parameters, such as exchange rates and interest rates, and then allows individual agents to play the game under the rules, such as firms that determine their own prices and output levels. So-called macroeconomic policy, under central planning, was actually designed so as to directly determine microeconomic outcomes. Such policy allowed Eastern Europe to achieve successes in specific areas (such as in heavy industry) but was ineffective for achieving overall satisfactory long-term economic performance. The costs of targeting specific areas at the expense of other areas is becoming increasingly apparent, as hidden inflation turns into open inflation, as the outmoded status of factories is revealed, as harm to the environment is documented, and so on. He warns that successful transition cannot be achieved without first creating certain institutional prerequisites, such as a sound financial system. Only then can the selective measures that currently constitute macroeconomic policy be replaced by macroeconomic policy in the Western sense of the word.

Milan Sojka addresses one of the thorniest issues facing all reforming Eastern European economies: the generation of unemployment during the transformation process. He divides the unemployment that will unfold into two types. Frictional unemployment will result as firms seek to become more efficient in the increasingly market-oriented environment and lay off the artificially employed. Structural unemployment will result as totally inefficient industries are eliminated from the Eastern European economies entirely. Warning that societies will tolerate only so much unemployment, he argues for measures to slow down the rate at which workers are released (such as the use of selective trade barriers to stagger the liquidation process), to stimulate new private sector jobs (especially in the service sector during the early phases of transition, since privatization of large enterprises will require more time), and to alleviate the conditions of those who do become unemployed (through the creation of a social safety net).

Andrej Kondratowicz and Jan Michalek focus our attention on the international dimensions of macroeconomic policy during transition. After summarizing the failed attempts by Polish authorities during the 1980s to bring balance to the foreign sector, they detail the specific foreign account measures adopted in 1990 as part of the so-called shock therapy, or Balcerowicz Plan, and examine the successes and failures brought on by these measures designed to open up the Polish economy. Behind the government's apparent success in building up a substantial trade surplus and foreign reserves, they argue, lies its failure to actively use the exchange rate (i.e., to revalue), which may have exacerbated the ensuing recession and inflation. The existence of such substantial foreign exchange reserves may make negotiations on debt reduction more difficult. They nonetheless conclude that radical reforms in the international arena, such as the introduction of limited convertibility in the Polish case, are critical to any centrally planned economy trying to accomplish serious reform.

Opening the section on the microeconomics of transition, Katalin Szabo discusses the importance of small ventures to the Hungarian economy in both the pre-1989 and post-1989 periods. Despite initial attempts in the post-World War II period to eliminate such enterprises, new and somewhat unusual forms of economic activity emerged with the initial reforms of 1968, and the proliferation of these new forms increased in number and importance in the early 1980s. In spite of official attitudes, which varied from supportive to oppressive over the period, the existence of these small firms spared Hungary many of the shortages that characterized other Eastern European countries. The small firms were a major source of growth of output and employment for the Hungarian economy of the 1980s. While certain unfavorable features (e.g., tax avoidance) have emerged in this sector, Szabo considers them to be an essential and dynamic feature of the new Hungary. Evidence that substantial foreign capital has been attracted to this sector provides additional support to the argument.

Mieczyslaw Socha and Urszula Sztanderska look at the ability of firms to adjust to the macro-level shock therapy program in Poland. Facing, for the first time, a lack of demand, many enterprises initially cut output and employment, raised prices (especially when they retained monopoly status), reduced borrowing and investment activities, and restrained wages even below the allowable limits. They then pressured government to loosen up on economic policy. As a result of some easing, inflation edged up but output stabilized at a low level. Moreover, labor productivity fell since output fell more than employment and new technologies were not brought on line. The authors argue that Polish firms are simply not equipped to operate in a market environment. Managers do not have appropriate and adequate skills, and even if they did, they are constrained by a dispersion of property rights among employee self-management councils, trade unions, and, sometimes, state authorities, by various legal restrictions, shortages of development funds, and so on. They conclude that more appropriate enterprise responses cannot be expected without more privatization. However, since privatization takes time, they call for greater management autonomy during the transition process.

Jerzy Wilkin focuses on the critical role of the agricultural sector and peasants in the systemic transformation of the Polish economy, both prior to the 1989 revolution and currently during its shock-therapy program. He argues that a large private farming sector survived the central planning era not because of its own internal strength but rather due to the weaknesses of the socialized sector. He generalizes this conclusion to other countries that experimented with central planning and social ownership. He then discusses the outlook for the farming sector during transition and warns that this sector is bearing the brunt of the transition process because it continues to operate as an island of private enterprise in a sea of state-owned enterprises, in Poland as well as in the other Eastern European countries. While he does not detail a plan for easing this burden, he does call for a speedy adjustment process.

Taken together, these chapters suggest that the mapping out of a successful transition process is very much an art. We should not be surprised if the standard, orthodox policy prescriptions do not work as expected. While several authors note the importance of timing and sequencing of policies, there is controversy over what constitutes the best and most desirable transformation process. The authors convince us that short-term miracles are unlikely, but they are not overly pessimistic about the long-term outlook. They prepare us for possible backsliding, as the short-term costs rise too high for some societies to bear, and for policy adjustments, as societies realize they have taken wrong turns or as superior paths become evident.

The reader should bear in mind that all of the chapters were written at the inception of transition and that while the past was fairly clear, the crystal balls for discerning the future are still quite cloudy. Several authors argued for, and no author objected to, foreign aid to ease the transition. However, foreign aid was never seen as the centerpiece of the changes.

The three countries examined most closely—Czechoslovakia, Hungary, and Poland—have each chosen different strategies. Generally speaking, Hungary is continuing a process begun more than 20 years ago but at a somewhat accelerated pace. Neither Czechoslovakia nor Poland experimented very extensively with reform prior to 1989, but now the former has decided to move relatively more slowly than the latter. The differing levels of development, imbalances, and foreign debt, as well as differing social and political contexts, may never allow us to determine conclusively the strengths and weaknesses of each overall strategy, but we may over time be able to select more or less desirable elements from within the strategies. The chapters in the volume clearly give us a better vantage point from which to view these history-making transitions.

Part I

The Transfer of Property Rights

Chapter 1

The Case for Privatization in Czechoslovakia and other Centrally Planned Economies

Jiri Hlavacek

The behavior of both the firm and the consumer is the basic characteristic of every economy. Their behavior is akin to the law of gravity in mechanics: They determine the direction of movement in space without barriers or external force.

Mainstream economic theory does not deal with the problems of the behavioral characteristics of firms and consumers to any great extent. It is simply assumed that firms wish to maximize profits, while consumers seek the maximization of utility. Other forms of behavior are simply dismissed as deviations from the norm.

The presumption of standard economic behavior is not an isolated assumption; rather, it is connected to other assumptions of neoclassical economics. The most important assumption of neoclassical analysis, as it pertains to this chapter, is the independence of the firm.

This independence, in Western market economies, takes for granted the idea that the firm has the right and the will to make its own decisions for its own purposes. No one beyond the firm is allowed to dictate to the firm, and the firm's position is determined only by its own decision making and by the conditions of the market. It is only the firm and the invisible hand of the marketplace that influence the firm's prosperity or failure.

A centrally planned economy (CPE) cannot be taken as an economic system with firms free to do what they wish. It is this basic tenet that separates the CPE from the Western market economy.

THE FIRM'S BEHAVIOR IN A CPE

In a centrally planned economy, there is no bankruptcy. All firms survive despite the fact that the majority of them are not vital.

In a CPE, the original sense of the word "market" does not exist. The output of one firm does not compete with that of other firms. All products find their customers, as a basic feature of the CPE is that demand exceeds supply.

While it may be difficult for those in market economies to understand why firms do not take advantage of this excess demand to increase their profits, the explanation lies in the objective function of the typical firm in the CPE. The reasoning applies to all socialist economies afflicted with central planning: Firms do not produce as much as is effectively possible; on the contrary, every firm in the CPE produces as little as is allowed.

In the Western market economy, the market plays the role of the supervisor. The firm that is not able to work under the constraints of the market and its budget does not survive.

The role of the market in the CPE is played by the planning authority. It is a special economic agent that simply does not exist in the market economy. The role of the planning authority in the CPE is above all microeconomic in nature. It influences the economic situations of all firms.

The CPE's planning authority judges the efficiency of every firm and assesses the plan for the firm. The plan becomes the low boundary of the firm's production set, that is, the lowest level of efficiency that the center takes for a sufficient level. This lower limit is not a single number; it is the statement (function) determining a volume of output according to a volume of input. Thus:

$$y \geq g(x)$$

where   y = volume of output

x = volume of inputs

g(x) = the planning constraint

The firm chooses the volume of input while the volume of output is predetermined by the center's statement $g(x)$.

The center does not have precise information about the production possibilities of every firm, because the firms have little reason to provide the center with this knowledge. Information about production efficiency of the firm would provide the center with more accurate information about the firms' production capabilities.

Because the center lacks information about the firms' production capabilities, it cannot distinguish the efficient from the inefficient firm. For this reason, the index method of planning prevails: The center determines the plan for the year t as a given percentage increase from the output levels of year t-1. Therefore, a firm that produced as efficiently as possible in year t-1 would probably not be able to fulfill the plan for the next year. The manager of such a firm would be replaced by the central authority. That is why managers with an efficiency-minimizing objective function survive. It is also the reason for the prevailing anti-efficient behavior of firms under a CPE.

In such an economic system, prices cannot provide information about the scarcity of resources used by the enterprises or of the products produced. The vicious cycle is closed: Firms are interested in inefficient production.

The *oeconomic man* in a CPE is quite different from *homo oeconomicus* from neoclassical economic theory. The typical socialist manager is closer to the model of *homo se assecurans*, that is, the "man securing himself."

A simplified, mathematically formulated model of a firm is indicated below. The model assumes reserve-maximizing behavior. Let:

$f(x)$ = production function

r = reserve

The reserve is the difference between a firm's production possibilities and its real volume of output:

$r(x,y) = f(x) - y$

Production set Y is limited from above by the production function, and from below by planning constraints.

$Y = \{(x,y) \ / \ g(x) \leq y \leq f(x)\}$

The optimal production situation (x,y) for the firm in a CPE can be expressed as a result of the following optimization:

$r = r(x,y) = \max r(x,y); xEY$

This optimization can be demonstrated as in Figure 1.1.

Note that prices play an insignificant role in decision making in a CPE. Prices do not influence a firm's behavior, and their only role is to help in the formulation of a planning constraint.

Figure 1.1
Production Function of a Firm Exhibiting Reserve-Maximizing Behavior

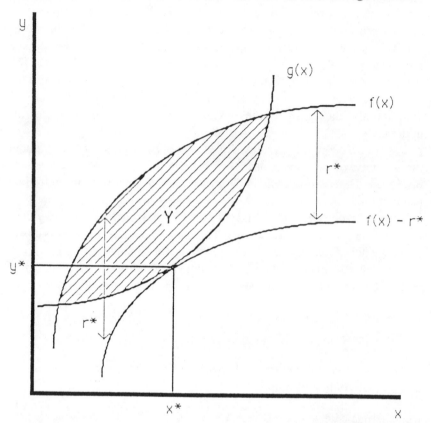

The difference between *homo oeconomicus* and *homo se assecurans* is evident from the following comparison: *Homo oeconomicus* (a neoclassical model of a profit-maximizing firm) has a production set given without prices by technological constraints, and prices are the parameters of its objective function. *Homo se assecurans*, in contrast, chooses an optimal production situation from the production set formulated with the help of prices, but the objective function is price independent.

Economic laws are very strong, rendering it difficult to construct the economic world according to the wishes of a "social engineer." The organized arrangement of an economy, and above all, the designated form of property rights, dooms the efforts of the social engineer. Thus, any attempt to make a socialist economy more efficient without changes in ownership relations cannot be successful.

Contemporary economic reform goes beyond the socialist arrangements existing in all of the countries of Eastern Europe. The reforms now provide the hope of crossing the Rubicon; however, there are and will continue to be obstacles and barriers. In the following section, the Czechoslovak experience will be briefly described and the consequences of moving into the new economic climate (into a system of new firm and consumer objective functions) will be forecast.

THE ECONOMIC CLIMATE IN CZECHOSLOVAKIA TODAY

Central planning in Czechoslovakia was formally cancelled in the autumn of 1990. While the central planning board no longer exists, a large majority of the nation's enterprises are still under state ownership.

The system of dictated prices was partially liberalized in the beginning of 1991. The economic ministers in Czechoslovakia today understand the destructive role of the system of centrally controlled prices. Without information from market prices, allocative efficiency cannot be achieved, the scarcity of resources cannot be recognized, and the utility of different products cannot be compared. These conclusions lead to the question of why the system of prices has not been completely liberalized. A rationale is presented below.

The only difference between a traditional CPE and the price liberalization CPE is in the firm's low boundary production set. The low boundary is formally expressed as a budget constraint, but it exhibits a significant difference. The budget constraint in a market economy is independent of the will of the other agents and represents the only information for the firm. In an economy with centrally controlled prices, this constraint expresses the center's evaluation of the efficiency of the particular firm. Once again, the firm places its inefficient production foot forward.

The firm does this because it knows that state ownership practically makes the demise of the firm impossible. Where the center limits prices, the firm fears the decreasing of the output price relative to the prices of the input. The center is under pressure from all firms to increase the prices of output. Once again, only the firm with significant reserves will most assuredly survive.

One can only hope that the total liberalization of prices will be the jump over the Rubicon, the leap over the barriers that separate the efficient from the inefficient firms. Unfortunately, this is not the case and the task is more difficult. Total price liberalization is not a sufficient condition for an efficient economic climate, as it can also be shown that with state owner-ship, an inefficient economic climate can arise even with free contractual prices.

Let us assume that there exist two enterprises under state ownership. The state is interested in the survival of both firms. Let it be further assumed that the output of the first represents the input of the second firm.

Under the above assumptions, one cannot exclude the conclusion that the survival (the fulfillment of the budget constraint) of the first firm is contingent upon a higher price of the commodity traded. The survival of the second firm is assured only when the price of its output exceeds the prices of its inputs. If this condition does not exist, the central authority is forced to subsidize either of the two firms.

As a result, both firms have an immediate interest in overstating their true costs and thus falsely portraying their operating conditions. In this way, both firms are granted a less restrictive budget and a higher proba-bility for survival. This type of strategy is followed by firms and leads to their inefficient behavior, which is continually observed.

In my opinion, the basic cause of the anti-efficient behavior of the firm is the paternalism of the center. When the center is interested in the survival of the firm, *homo oeconomicus* has little chance to exist and multiply. The necessary condition for a profit-maximizing economic climate is to cancel state ownership.

I have indicated two conditions necessary to revive the sick economies of the former socialist countries. The first is price liberalization, and the second is the radical restriction of state ownership.

The Czechoslovak path to a market economy emphasizes the second condition. While price liberalization in Czechoslovakia, in comparison with the other former socialist countries, is only partial, the privatization process is moving more rapidly.

This method of crossing the Rubicon is, in my opinion, the more hopeful. Although the privatization process is the slower of the two, I believe it will result in the quickest way to efficiency in production.

This does not mean that the privatization path is not without danger. The process requires relatively stable prices and therefore some level of price control. The current leaders of the Czechoslovak economy want to keep prices centrally determined only to a limited degree. The possibility of this is, however, doubtful. The producers of price-controlled commod-ities will be endangered by the increasing cost of input prices. This, in turn, will require more widespread price controls. A second danger cannot be neglected. Central price control gives the center significant power, and future price liberalization militates against that power. It is this latter concern that strongly argues for a healthy democratic political climate.

In the Czechoslovak system, there will be firms with mixed private and state ownership. In the first years, state ownership will prevail and central price control will play an important role. This is also the reason that profit maximization will not prevail.

The Czechoslovak path to the market economy, as stated above, gives privatization priority over full price liberalization. The leaders of Czechoslovak economic reform have taken this route out of fear of rapid inflation. More importantly, in the long run, this path will lead directly and continuously toward a profit-maximizing economic climate. This will occur during the transition to a full market economy, and the failure of specific firms cannot be excluded. It is assumed that firms will minimize the danger of having to close, and this will ensure some level of economic success based on the principle of the survival of the fittest. The process will be gradually transformed from *homo se assecurans* to that of profit maximization.

It cannot be conclusively argued that privatization is more important than price liberalization. Both elements of reform are important. It appears, however, that price liberalization under the conditions of state ownership cannot play the most significant role. Privatization, however, enables a reasonable price liberalization as well as changes in the economic climate. In this sense, privatization is the primary vehicle for the economic transformation of a CPE.

Chapter 2

The Role of Property Rights in the Transition in Hungary

Zoltan Bara

It is widely accepted among economists that the most important characteristic by which different economic systems have been classified is property rights. Traditionally, the classification of economic systems has been in terms of "isms," such as capitalism and socialism, in which the nature of the property rights distinguishes each system. We can easily describe a particular economy by using the property rights approach, even if statistical data are insufficient. Such is the case in the economic transition in Hungary in the last three years.

The changes in forms of property rights were so unusual and impressive during that period that we can grasp the nature of the transition only by analyzing the newly developed ownership forms. I cannot provide exact numbers on how many firms have undergone transitions, as data do not exist. Since we have only rough estimates, those who care only about "hard" statistics will be disappointed. But those who are interested in views, opinions, descriptions, and possibilities may find this chapter interesting.

Property is a bundle of rights or set of relations between people with regard to some thing.[1] The division of ownership rights into three broad types will help us describe the transition process in detail.[2] First is the disposition of the object in question—the transfer of ownership rights to others. Second, ownership may or may not include the right to utilization, whereby the owner can use the object in question in any manner. Third, ownership may or may not imply the right to dispose of or consume the products and/or services generated by the object in question. Distinguishing among these three types of ownership is a necessary tool for comprehending the transition in Hungary from a centrally planned economy to a market-oriented system.

HISTORICAL BACKGROUND: THE ECONOMIC REFORM

This transition began 23 years ago with the introduction of the New Economic Mechanism (NEM) in 1968. The reasons behind the reform program were very similar to those of other socialist countries in this region that have also developed some kinds of reform. They include: the Soviet type of industrialization, overcentralization, extensive growth, rigid plan mechanism, and the lack of real incentives.[3]

The main objective of NEM was to combine central directions with responsibilities for upper-level administrative agencies and the directors of enterprises. The first change was a significant reduction in the number of directives coming from the central authorities. The enterprises were allowed to respond to the forces of supply and demand; most of the enterprises were to be freed from compulsory output targets. The decreasing direct administrative controls would be replaced by "economic regulators," which included price policy, investment policy, credit policy, and fiscal policy. The purpose of these regulators was to allow enterprise autonomy but to keep their activities within bounds acceptable to the central authorities.[4]

The reform brought changes in some property rights that had been totally under state ownership to the industrial sectors. Before NEM, only the state had property rights in resource allocation, as well as in the utilization of the production resources and in the disposition of products and services. As a result of NEM, enterprises were given rights in the decision-making process for managing themselves within the bounds of regulations. They independently decided what to produce, to what extent, and in what variety. They made the decisions on the use of profit, whether to invest or to increase wages. But they didn't have the rights to establish or eliminate a firm. Those rights remained with the state authorities. Thus, we might say that the first basic property rights—the disposition of a firm—remained "public," that is, in the hands of authorities. Most of the other rights went to individuals, in particular to the managers of the basically state-owned enterprises, and therefore became "private."

It is also correct to say that the newly formed heterogeneous property rights structure was not simply a mix of public and private property, because the division of the property rights was not unambiguous. It was not based on formal agreements or contracts between the state and the managers. The managers were not allowed to freely seek their own interests, but they did so. The state officials were not allowed to intervene in the matters of form, but they did so. Thus, the division of property rights was partly formal, but to a greater extent, informal. Many informal "gentlemen's agreements" between the state and firms formed the bargaining process on the overall plan and the local plan. Therefore, the private rights in management decision making were not really private, and state ownership did not yield purely public or central decisions. The lack of an open and unambiguous division of property rights, and the scope of the informal bargains and relations has been one of the most important factors in the failures of the reform.

CHANGES IN THE REFORM PROCESS IN THE 1970s AND 1980s

The implementation of NEM encountered three main difficulties:

1. Political constraints. First, Soviet concerns limited the extent to which central control over key production factors could be replaced by individual decision making.[5] Although it was widely recognized that the reform process should be extended to the political sphere as a compromise between the economists and the politicians, the Communist Party leadership remained untouched.

2. Domestic economic constraints. The reform was implemented in a unique sort of industrial structure. The Hungarian industrial enterprises went through a strong, centrally directed wave of mergers in the early 1960s. The underlying rationale was the belief that fewer enterprises would be easier to control than many. As a result, Hungary had not developed intermediate-size enterprises.[6] This meant an oligopolistic industrial structure, in which the central authorities could "talk" to enterprises rather easily, because of their limited number. Moreover, a planned socialist system typically operates under policy goals different from those of market capitalist systems. According to Granick (1975), in the Hungarian case, the three most distinguishing policy objectives were: (a) maintaining full employment; (b) intolerance of inflation; and (c) the lack of desire for sharply expanded mobility of the labor force.[7]

3. International economic recession. The sharp changes in world oil prices in the early 1970s made it necessary to connect external and internal prices on a permanent basis, but the adjustments of internal prices and the revaluation of the Hungarian currency have kept internal price increases much below the external price increases. The result was an overconsumption of oil and, together with other factors, a large foreign debt.[8] The terms of trade with both

the West and COMECOM (Council for Mutual Economic Assistance) countries turned sharply against Hungary in the mid-1970s. The result was a growing annual external deficit and an accumulating external hard currency debt.

Hungarian economic policy, in trying to face those constraints, was directed toward maintaining the standard of living and bringing the trade balance under control. As mentioned previously, the NEM used economic regulators as directives. Therefore, any intended improvement should have used these tools to introduce a new regulation or alter an old one. As both Hungarian and Western observers emphasized, Hungarian industrial enterprises were operating under thousands of regulations that were implemented by not only the planners and state agencies but the banking system as well. Moreover, firms were protected by the wide range of subsidies.[9]

This system might be called one of "simulation of market," because the declared goal of most regulators was to simulate the effect of a real market system. An artificial price system would replace the effect of international competition, and a new form of state-ownership would achieve more efficiency in the long run.

STATE-OWNED ENTERPRISE WITH COMPANY BOARD

By the beginning of the 1980s, it was clear, even for the political leaders, that there were no long-term interests connected to the utilization of state-owned enterprises. It was said that the reason for the inefficient, loss-making management was the lack of long-term ownership interests. Within the overall original objectives of NEM, many specialists were asked to take part in one of the numerous committees, the tasks of which were to elaborate a new concept of "socialist" property ownership and management.

They realized that ownership decisions must be separated from the government and state, but that seemed to be infeasible within the framework of the constitution. The basic part of ownership rights belonged to the ruling party and its agencies, which should have been practicing those rights together with the local and the central authorities, and partly with top managers of the firms. The problem was that no persons or institutions had a real interest in the long-run profitable utilization of the firms. The state as an owner was a mere abstraction, a fiction without the intentions and/or power to accomplish those property rights. The committees outlined three possible ownership organizations which had been proved to be viable:

1. holding companies, mutual funds, which were working in developed market systems,
2. self-managing collective ownership, which has worked as a dominant form in the Yugoslavian economy, but not in an unquestionably efficient fashion,
3. corporative-like institutions, wherein an economy is governed by collective political bargains between the state and the organizations of the employees and employers. These have been working well in Austria and Sweden.

The final decision was for the corporative form[10] but not without compromises. The decision seemed to be reasonable considering Hungarian economy and politics. The essence of corporative property rights is to reconcile the differing interests represented by the main organizations, institutions, and the state. After negotiations, the reconciled mutual interests would serve as property rights. This would have been nothing more than the legalization of the ongoing informal communications between the top managers and state representatives.

At least that was the idea, but it did not work. The materialized form of the company board was closer to the formerly discarded collective ownership than to the corporative one. The reasons were twofold. First, under Communist Party leadership, people had given up taking part in political matters. Thus, there were no institutions representing individual or group interests, either for the employers or for the employees.[11]

The second reason for the basic failure of the original concept of the company board was a more practical one. The number of people on a company board could be no less than five and no more than fifty-one. Half of its members would be elected by the employees, and not more than one-third of them would be assigned by the director. The rest of the members were representatives of state agencies. Thus, the founding state or party agency could not count on a majority. The only legal tool of the party leader or of other representatives on the board was persuasion. Those people were not used to rejections and did not want to take the risk of being turned down. Therefore, the party and the authorities were reluctant to send representatives to the boards. Instead, they continued to use informal channels, not without success, and special rights[12] to reach their goals.

Thus, in most cases the company board became an imitation of a corporative decision-making council. In practice, the company boards have worked as a quasi-collective ownership. The board appoints and dismisses directors and makes decisions about investments, mergers, and the use of profits. The most important drawback of this property form is that it represents the interests of employees instead of the profit-oriented owner. The company board has not brought real changes and consequently has not yielded any improvements in the efficiency and flexibility of the socialist enterprises. To answer these deficiencies, the first step was the "spontaneous privatization" in the late 1980s. But one might consider it as directly following on the above-mentioned "spontaneous" form of property rights.

THE ORIGINS OF SPONTANEOUS PRIVATIZATION

This sort of privatization is unique, as it means real changes in the form of state property rights without creating real private ownership. Spontaneous privatization is a process by which firms get rid of state ownership without payment or significant compensation. Before we explore this subject, let us take into consideration a natural question: How could the situation have gotten this far under the communist era?

The answer is that spontaneous privatizations sprang from the development of the Hungarian reform process itself. If readers have grasped the reasons that led to a quasi-market situation, including quasi-collective ownership and the company boards, they will see a special economic environment in which everyone believed in the forces of market, but no one thought that a real market economy could ever be achieved because of socialism. Even the majority of the political leaders believed this. This belief appeared in both political and professional speeches and in common conversations. Whenever anything went wrong in the economy, the lack of market forces would be blamed for it.

As we have argued, the company board did not offer a real solution to the long-term concern of profitability. Again, the reason was the lack of real private owners. But private ownership of the basic production resources was incompatible with the socialist constitution, which allowed only public ownership. How could the problem be solved? The answer was two new laws, the Company Act and the Transformation Act.

These two acts, although issued after the last communist government, had been prepared and developed under the Grosz government. At that time, the government realized that the central political leadership was too weak to take control over the socialist enterprises. Having seen that the company board was not a solution, they thought only one way remained: to sign away the rest of the basic state property rights without the declared admission that it would mean private ownership. Does there seem to be a contradiction? There was.

THE ESSENCE OF SPONTANEOUS PRIVATIZATION

The two acts made it possible for firms to get rid of the last remains of state ownership. The procedure was simple but not always fair or public. Let's suppose that we are two managers of a large, loss-making socialist enterprise called Ganz-Mavag. Ganz-Mavag has one or two relatively good, profitable subunits and a few other plants or other subunits that have been suffering losses. We and some other managers might think that the only way to avoid bankruptcy is to transform Ganz-Mavag into another company and get rid of the loss-making units or, if that is not possible, to reorganize them.

According to the Company Act, the new property forms can be a company with limited liabilities or simply a share-holding company—but an original "socialist" creature and not a Western type. In an expensive project, the managers submit their enterprise to an evaluation made by a special consulting company. As a result of this evaluation, we, as managers of Ganz-Mavag, would be given an estimated value of our plants and subunits. Let's suppose that it is one million forints. In an optimal case, the consulting company might give us some suggestions concerning the reorganization of the loss-making units, or just simply advise us to sell them. As we will see, avoiding losses is not the essence of this sort of transformation.

After obtaining the estimated value, we (or the consulting company) put together a transformation plan. First, we may plan to create two or three independent share-holding companies from the better plants of the former socialist enterprise. These former units become self-managing companies under different names. Who is going to get their shares?

These shares, in whole or in part, go to a financial holding company. In our fictional case, the Ganz-Mavag has become a mere financial holding company, which holds the shares of its former subunits. The Ganz-Mavag could sell its plants or other properties, even the shares. The holding company's only task is to make sure that the new independent companies will make profits instead of losses.

But who is going to buy a share? It is a part of the "socialist" sort of solution: nobody, for two reasons. First, at that time (in 1988 and 1989), individuals were not allowed to buy or sell shares. Only legal persons, that is, banks, firms, and other institutions, had the right to purchase and own shares. In other words, there was no real market for investment capital. Second, the face value of those shares is imaginary, having nothing to do with the real value of the firms' assets. Therefore, the shares were unlikely to be sold, even if there were a market for them. In most cases, a controlling package of shares went to the holding company and the rest to banks or other creditors who were willing to give credits to the newly formed companies.

Let's analyze the situation after the transformation. We have the former Ganz-Mavag as a financial holding company that can manage these equities by trading them and invest in other profitable businesses. The Ganz-Mavag owns a million-forint value of shares of the newly formed companies. Those companies are independent and free from state directions; they are no longer state-owned firms. But what about Ganz-Mavag itself? It is still a state property, at least formally. This means that the state or the government could control its former plants through this financial holding company. The transformation must be continued by another trick: the transformation of the Ganz-Mavag into a share company.

We may ask who made the decision about the transformation of a state firm in the first place. If the firm were already operating under a company board, the decision concerning the transition would be made by this council. Let's suppose our firm, Ganz-Mavag, was transformed into a holding company by the decision of its board. (If a firm had no company board, the decision would be made by its director with the permission of the founding authorities.) The number of people on the board and its membership must change following the first transition. It is quite probable that although the number of employees of the original Ganz-Mavag, as a social enterprise, was many thousands, the number of employees of the transformed Ganz-Mavag is just a few dozen.[13] This changed board can again make a new decision about another transformation into the form of a share-holding company.

Who is going to own the shares of this newly transformed holding company? Since the market for capital shares is thin and can only go into the hands of legal persons, the would-be owners are likely to be the founding authorities, together with banks and other creditors. The face or issuing value of the shares of this holding company has nothing to do with the assessed value of one million, but can be much higher or even lower. The potentially profitable operations of this holding company are making new investments, lending to other firms, or trading shares. The distribution of the shares is a matter of bargaining power. Because of the relative weakness of the central and local authorities, only a small part of the shares might go to them; the majority might go to banks and/or the employees of the company.

Let's summarize the results of these transitions.

1. The property rights concerning the disposition of resources have been trans-
    formed, partly or completely, from state authorities to shareholders. The
    shareholders are not real persons; rather, there now exists a distribution of
    property rights among institutions (banks, creditors, other firms, and author-
    ities). The most important change is that the formerly informal property
    relations have become open and have remained mostly in the same hands—of
    the same top managers of the former state firms, of upper-level civil servants,
    and of former party officials.
2. There has been no significant change in the inner structure of production,
    technology, management techniques, and product qualities.
3. We can witness that a new economic dominant class has been forming: The
    top executives of banks and holding companies become more powerful
    because of the series of connections, mergers, and transitions of the state
    firms. They have almost uncontrolled power in decision making.[14]

One of the most contradictory characteristics of privatization in Hungary is the role of employee participation. The campaign of privatization
has been accompanied from the beginning by the declaration that the more
shares purchased by the employees, the better. To implement this goal,
easy payment plans were introduced. However, most of the employees
were not interested because, having no market for stocks, what could they
do with the shares? The employees' purchase of shares had no significant
effect on the process of privatization.

ARGUMENTS FOR AND AGAINST SPONTANEOUS PRIVATIZATION

Most Western observers have condemned spontaneous privatization for
two reasons: first, because of the "parachuting" possibilities, and second,
because of the lack of appropriate compensation payments to the government. They complain about this "poor solution" but keep forgetting two
important things: that privatization must be completed quickly and that the
whole country has been suffering from a chronic lack of capital. Thus, the
process of privatization cannot be carried out in a Western way. Selling a
firm would take a lot of precious time, and Hungary cannot afford to waste
time. Spontaneous privatization has provided solutions for both drawbacks.

It is true that many officials, managers, directors, and leaders assigned
by the former communist regime have successfully preserved their positions by taking part in the directory board or supervisory board of one or
two newly formed share-holding companies. However, most of the best
Hungarian managers can be found within that circle of former "communists."

As far as the government payment problem is concerned, for a better understanding we must know a little more about the general positions and feelings of the top managers in 1988 and 1989. The top managers of the biggest firms had perceived a vacuum of political power and felt the disintegration of the government. The informal connections between the top managers and the government had been weakening rapidly since the resolutions of the Communist Party in 1988. By 1989, the system of regulations based on the simulation of market had been totally wrecked, and no other sort of coordination—especially not the market—had replaced it. The top managers felt abandoned although they had never felt much freedom from governmental paternalism in their decisions.

The Company Act and, later, the Transformation Act have strengthened the formerly informal property rights in managers' hands, both legally and politically. The state-party was disorganized and the government was compelled to hand the remaining property rights to the top managers in order to temporarily maintain the ability of the economy to function. Thus, spontaneous privatization can be considered as some kind of reward that was given in completely legal ways. One could question the fairness of these actions, but that is another matter.

WESTERN VIEWS OF SOCIALIST PRIVATIZATION

The privatization of a socialized industry has been a popular topic among Western economists for a long time. There have been a number of governmental programs in developed countries concerning privatization of a nationalized enterprise or of a whole industry.[15] The subject of privatization became particularly interesting when applied to some socialist countries. The views and ideas related to socialist privatization are many and are based on different perceptions and values. The majority of them are far from being introduced and implemented. They are basically suggestions for different nationwide experiments, and they do not recognize that the people in these countries are exhausted from the nationwide experiments provided by the former communist regimes. However, it is worthwhile to take a quick glance into the most characteristic views.

One of the most common concepts is the notion of "egalitarian socialist privatization" introduced by, among others, Edgar Feige, who initially presented his paper at an international conference held in Moscow in 1989.[16] According to Feige, the Soviet Union should engage in a massive and rapid privatization by selling state enterprises, collectives, apartments, and land. This wave of privatization should be carried out in an egalitarian fashion to win popular support. Equity is supposed to be achieved by selling each citizen "equal fractional ownership in each and every state enterprise." The selling price "must be set low in order to assure a high real rate of return on the assets in order to provide sufficient incentives for citizens to voluntarily participate in the nationwide program" (Feige 1990: 26).

James Millar, a critic of Feige's view, has pointed out that as long as the government wants to seek the social goal of equity through privatization, the result would do nothing but "mimic the capitalist economy" (Millar 1990:65) and would lack the appropriate incentives both on the investment and the production side.

Other economists, like Michael Marrese, consider foreign participation in the process as the most important factor of privatization. Marrese argued that a forced, egalitarian or unequal, distribution of property rights among people would give foreign capital a supporting role instead of a leading role (Marrese 1990: 59). Privatization in every socialist country will need foreign investment, not just to compensate for the shortage of domestic capital, but for the sophisticated technology, well-educated management, and necessary foreign connections on the world markets. A forced majority of domestic ownership within each company would not provide enough incentive for foreign services, as most foreign capital is interested in majority or complete ownership.

As many observers have pointed out, the process of traditional privatization suffers from at least two major drawbacks: the evaluation problem and the lack of purchasing power. Enterprises need to be valued before they can be sold; otherwise, buyers and sellers cannot set sensible prices. It is not just that the information required for this task takes time to gather, but in most cases it cannot be obtained in appropriate forms. Moreover, the sources for information are not always dependable. Second, regardless of how worthless many of the state enterprises may be, the people lack the purchasing power to buy them up.

The *Economist* asks: Why not sell them abroad? The reason is simply that it would take precious time when it should be done quickly. The correct conclusion, according to the *Economist*, is to give them to the people in a form of portfolio capital (not, as Feige suggested, in equal proportion to the employees of each enterprise). The proposal is to create ten or so huge, state-owned holding companies and to divide the enterprises among them, though not necessarily in equal portions. Then, equal shares in the holding companies could be given to every adult. Thus, the holding companies would become like mutual funds. People would be free to trade shares and the managers both of holding companies and of enterprises would face immediate pressure to maximize the value of the assets in their charge.

The proposal is an interesting suggestion and seems to answer the problem of what should happen to the shares of the holding companies. However, this solution would require a well-defined role for government. Most Western observers seemed not to notice that the former socialist countries lack not just strong markets, but strong governments or states as well.[17] Without a strong state, any nationwide plan would be just another example of bureaucratic fiddling.

We cannot afford not to discuss the comments of the best-known Hungarian economist, Janos Kornai, who teaches at Harvard. He also can be considered a Western observer. His points are completely different from those of most Hungarians. The typical Hungarian is happy with the strengthening of market forces on the one hand and the fall of the bureaucratic state ownership on the other. According to Kornai (Kornai 1990), the most disgraceful aspect of the privatization concepts is their urgency. Why is there a hurry, he asks, to sell precious state assets at ridiculously low prices? If the answer is to avoid the inefficient operations of the state firms, Kornai would advocate another solution. Real public control over state enterprises would force them to operate more efficiently. What is needed, he argues, is a strong, public-oriented, controlled state. The state has to improve the performance of its firms before selling them.

It is hard to comment on Kornai's point because theoretically he is right, of course. But given the circumstances of Hungary, I think that the request for a strong government would not be too popular and could increase the chances of a political breakdown. Our solution is to choose from two evils, and the spontaneous privatization is the lesser one.

THE ROLE OF THE STATE PROPERTY AGENCY

The last government (Nemeth) before the collapse of the communist system tried to get back pieces of the property rights squandered by the Grosz government. The majority of the new and reborn parties have put pressure on officials to stop the spontaneous privatization, but mainly for political rather than economic reasons. The Nemeth government set up a new institution, the State Property Agency (SPA), to control the privatization.

The guidelines of SPA, among others, were to determine the range and circle of the would-be privatized industries, to achieve a proper evaluation of assets, to hasten foreign investments in order to diminish the huge governmental debts, and to set limits for the possible allowances to be given to employees of the privatized firms to buy shares. In sum, the main tasks of the SPA are twofold: to control spontaneous privatization by deciding on submitted cases and to generate centrally initiated privatization programs.

Note that the first task does not mean a halt to the spontaneous, self-managing transitions, as the government knew very well that without them, the goal of privatization (to cut the portion of state ownership radically) could not be accomplished. The SPA has permitted 77 transactions (from approximately 100) in which state firms had taken their assets into a company form according to the Company Act or the Transformation Act by November 1990. The most well-known case of the centrally initiated privatization program was the introduction of Ibusz to the Vienna exchange in the summer of 1990.

The process of spontaneous privatization has been accompanied by scandals, even after the establishment of the SPA. The repeated transformation of Apisz, then Dunaholding Co., would be the best example in 1989. Those scandals were just fuss without fire, generated by the opponent parties for political reasons. They were merely attempts of the central powers to get back the former property rights. The scandals were caused mainly by the difficulties in evaluating properties and by the inexperience of the Registrar of Companies and the courts. In March 1990, the Supreme Court nullified, retroactively, the selling of Hungarhotels to Swedish buyers, causing terrible damage to the credibility of the government's intention to draw in foreign capital. The SPA did not approve the selling of the famous Gerbaud-building (referring to an under-evaluation) and also rejected the privatization of Amfora for similar reasons.

By and large, the role of SPA can be considered a positive one. By the middle of 1990, the economic environment of privatization had significantly changed. The basic institutions for capital markets had begun to be established: a two-tier banking system, the partial liberation of the money market, the establishment of the Hungarian stock exchange, the strengthening of the legal system. Most important of all, a freely elected parliament had come to power and a new government (Antall) had started to operate. In this new environment, the process of spontaneous privatization must continue to be carried out within reasonable limits. The SPA does not prohibit spontaneous privatization, but rather tries to accomplish timely and necessary interventions. Without those interventions, the government would lose its only chance to cut the enormous deficit and debt.

The government faces a very hard dilemma concerning retroactive actions against the already privatized companies. It has to intervene somehow, because no one represented the public interests in the formerly closed, spontaneous privatizations. As a result of those transformations, a small group of people received unfairly generous material advantages without any payments to the state. On the other hand, by the time of the establishment of SPA, the majority of the large and mid-sized enterprises has already gone through some kind of transition, in a completely legal way. Therefore, any retroactive action would be but renationalization. Renationalization in order to obtain privatization? What a contradiction! Reconsidering legally closed cases would cause more damage to the general transition of the economy to a market-driven form than some questionable advantage from it.

ESTIMATIONS ON THE MAGNITUDE OF THE PRIVATIZATION

The extent of the public sector to be privatized is about 2,200 enterprises, with a combined value of 1,800 billion forints. Up to the end of 1989, about 500 state firms (with a value of about 10 billion forints, according to a non-official estimation) had gone through some transitions in a "spontaneous" form. For comparison, the foreign debt of Hungary is about 1,470 billion forints (U.S. $21 billion).

The first package of the SPA privatization program was announced in September 1990 and covered 20 companies with a combined asset-value of 33 billion forints. The average annual revenues of these firms had been 93 billion forints in 1989. The project is to be accomplished within two years. The situation is similar in the case of small-scale retail shops and restaurants, the privatization of which had been announced earlier as a project of "pre"-privatization.

The government has more recently announced a second package of centrally initiated privatization, which includes 23 additional state enterprises. The government's declared goal is to decrease the proportion of state ownership from 90 percent to 50 percent within three years.

CONCLUSION

The World Bank is deeply concerned about the acceleration of transformation in the former socialist countries, including Hungary. As a result, the office of the prime minister has elaborated a framework in which all state firms should be transformed into share-holding companies and the shares should be distributed immediately among the self-governing boards and the employees. This questionable concept involves that office, indicating the contradictory development of the privatization process.[18]

Nevertheless, it is widely believed among economists that a real market has begun for capital and privatized state assets. Therefore, privatization should continue along these lines. It would be a severe mistake to destroy the self-managing company boards and to stop the process of spontaneous privatization, because it would open avenues for unlimited governmental arbitrary actions and interventions to which privatization is opposed. Of course, it is necessary to create appropriate conditions in terms of legal requirements and public control that exclude or at least diminish the chances of abuse and mistakes. The SPA has been operating according to these goals and there is no reason to believe that we need to open an entirely new way for privatization.

The success of privatization is closely related to the chances of an economic breakthrough in the short run, as well as in the long run. A successful short run would mean, among other things, a decrease in foreign debt to a bearable level by revenue from privatization. However, it would probably not be enough to solve the foreign debt problem. The country is not going to succeed without aid from the developed world. In the long run, the goal of privatization is to establish a market economy based on private ownership. Thus, we can say the success of transition in Eastern Europe depends on the success of privatization. It must remain among our primary objectives.

NOTES

1. According to Montias (1976: 116), "the word ownership refers to an amalgam of rights that individuals may have over objects or claims on objects."

2. See, for example, Gregory and Stuart (1989: 10–11).

3. The most frequently cited book on this subject is Kornai (1959).

4. For example, just one-fifth of the prices were free, three-fifths were set within given limits, and the rest were centrally set. The decentralized investments were financed partly from the state budget. Wage policy would be within the overall policy goal of full employment. For details, see Robinson 1973.

5. It is enough to think of the suppression of Czechoslovakia's attempt to get rid of Soviet influence in 1968.

6. By 1970, there were only 812 industrial enterprises with an average of seven plants each. See Granick (1975: 224).

7. Ibid., p. 221.

8. See Csikos-Nagy (1978: 543).

9. For Westerners, see Gregory and Stuart (1989: 325) and Hewett (1981). For the Easterners see Tardos (1981).

10. How the negotiations among the numerous committees came to an end would be another long story. It was said, for example, that in the first stage, the

concept of holding companies had been the "front runner," but after a short conversation with two of the most famous Soviet economists, the holding company concept was taken off the agenda. After completing their study of the suggestions only one short question was asked: "Sto znacsit holding?" (What does holding mean?). At that time, that was enough for the political leaders. No one talked about holding companies afterward.

11. The trade unions were only attendants of the party.

12. One of these special rights was the veto of "basic" matters. And, of course, the decisions as to what qualified as "basic" were made by them.

13. That's why the economists call a financial holding company an "emptied property center."

14. The real danger behind this development is that the interests interlocked between the industrial and banking sectors can make it impossible for the credit and monetary system to fulfill its real job: financing the industries strictly on an economic basis. As indicative of this problem, we can see that the newly formed companies, similar to the socialist enterprises in the communist era, rarely had to face credit disapprovals.

15. One of the most frequently cited books on this subject is Vickers (1988).

16. The paper was published in 1990. See Feige (1990).

17. One of the few who has noticed is John Kenneth Galbraith, who stated in one of his lectures that what Eastern Europe really needed is not capitalism but a modern state. See Galbraith (1990).

18. The activity of this newly formed governmental institute led to problems within the government and to the resignation of the minister of finance, Ferenc Rabar, and finally to the elimination of this office at the beginning of 1991.

Chapter 3

Poland's Property Rights Problem in the Transition

Maciej Iwanek

PROPERTY RIGHTS IN THE COMMAND ECONOMY IN POLAND

Main Features

The preponderance of state ownership over other forms of property was the main characteristic of property rights in Poland during the last forty years. State ownership was supplemented to some extent with cooperative ownership, while private property was rather marginal in non-agricultural branches of economy. In 1987, the state owned 80.9 percent of all fixed assets outside agriculture, while the share of cooperative ownership was 10.5 percent, and that of private ownership was 8.3 percent.

In agriculture, the situation was different. In 1987, private farmers owned 72.3 percent of all fixed assets and 71.8 percent of the land. The position of private property in Polish agriculture, for reasons mentioned later in this chapter, was an exception in communist countries (excluding Yugoslavia).

Thus, the command economy in Poland was accompanied by a characteristic hierarchy of forms of property: state ownership as the principal form, the cooperative sector as a subsidiary one, and private property as a residual form.

A second feature of property rights characteristic to the command economy was strict state control of all non-state forms of ownership. First, the state controlled the price mechanism. It set prices, wages, and interest rates and allocated rationed resources (bank loans, foreign exchange, machinery, energy, etc.). Second, the state limited direct property rights, that is, the rights to possess, sell, and buy property and the rights to revenue from the property. For instance, farmers were not allowed to buy more than 20 hectares, or, 49.4 acres, of land. Also, cooperative ownership was strictly controlled by the state. As a result, cooperative ownership operated in a manner similar to that of the state sector. For this reason, and also for some ideological considerations referred to later, the data for both sectors of ownership are usually lumped together as one "socialized" sector.

Another characteristic feature of property rights of the command economy in Poland was that decision making was very poorly defined. Decisions concerning the use of property (state-owned or cooperative) were made in a very complicated process involving many tiers of the command hierarchy. This hierarchy was complex not only because the economy was managed from many tiers of the central government (trusts, ministries, planning commission, council of ministries, parliament), but also because this multilevel governmental hierarchy was intertwined with the Communist Party hierarchy. Many important economic decisions were taken by members of the party apparatus in an informal way. Strictly speaking, such decisions were illicit because they were not sanctioned by the law imposed by the communist government itself. This feature perhaps explains why it was so difficult to determine how important "ownership" decisions were made.[1] Consequently, it is hard to assign blame for the manifest squandering of public resources.

Origins

Several factors contributed to the property rights structure of the Polish command economy.

A command economy is not feasible unless private property is reduced to a marginal role. A command economy is molded as a single hierarchical organization, and the commanding heights of the economy issue orders and distribute the resources needed to carry out these orders. This means that property rights must be concentrated where commands originate. It would be impossible to administer by means of commands economic agents that own their own resources and dispose of their income. Therefore, it was inevitable that the state became the ultimate owner of economic resources. The parallel development of the central planning structure and of the state ownership of resources was not a historical accident.

But Poland was not only a country with a command economy; it was also a country in which a totalitarian dictatorship was attempted.[2] Such a dictatorship is not feasible in a society with classes and groups that, in earning a living, are independent from the ruling elite. Therefore, in addition to economic grounds, there were strong political grounds for eliminating the middle classes by stripping them of their economic base, that is, of private property. This explains why the ruling communists were hostile even to very small private possessions and businesses. Thus, the struggle against private farms, shops, restaurants, and barbers had, in part, a political basis.

At the same time, an ideological justification for this property structure was developed. The ruling ideology included a ranking of different forms of property according to so-called ideals of socialist society. The socialist society, to be achievable in some undetermined future, was to be based on the "social ownership of means of production." Official ideologues interpreted this vague term as designating ownership exercised by the central government in the name of "the whole society." Consequently, "socialist ownership" was plainly identified with state ownership. According to the ideological yardstick that was common in the past, the more extensive state ownership, the better, because the economy was that much closer to the ideal.[3] Cooperative property was considered an inferior form of ownership, as compared with state ownership, because it was not ownership by "the whole society," but "group ownership." In some ideological interpretations, cooperative ownership was a temporary form of property in transition from private to fully socialist property.

Both state and cooperative property were regarded in the official ideology as superior to private ownership, which was considered a relic of the previous capitalist society and was expected to disappear in a fully developed socialist system. However, a distinction was made between private possession of consumer goods (clothes, furniture, TV sets, etc., which were called "personal property" to give the distinction semantic support) and "private ownership of means of production." The former was regarded as compatible with "socialist principles," whereas the latter was not. This ideological valuation of different forms of ownership served as a justification for different policies among sectors.

Some historical reasons specific to the political situation in Poland also contributed to molding the property rights structure. The distinct position of private ownership in agriculture is explained by these factors. Polish peasantry still had a strong, independent political representation in the first years of communist rule. Therefore, the process of forced collectivization started in Poland with some delay and never gained the impetus it had in other communist countries. A faction of Polish communists, which came to power after Stalin's death with Gomulka as their leader, preferred the evolutionary and voluntary process of collectivization. Being additionally motivated by strong popular demands, they accepted the dissolution of *kolkhozs*, which had been established in the beginning of the 1950s.

Economic Consequences

The above-described property rights, characterized by the predominance of state ownership and state control of all kinds of property, contributed much to the failures of the command economy. The command economy in communist countries brought about the waste of resources and negligence of existing productive assets, lags in technological progress, and so on. The property rights of the command economy contributed to these failures mainly because they made any effective system of economic incentives impossible.

First, the abolition of private property eliminates high-powered incentives typical of the market, since these incentives are based on exclusive appropriation of net income streams by independently operating agents. Therefore, the command economy is almost completely stripped of strongly motivated actors, who are replaced by agents working for the state mono-hierarchy.[4]

Even where low-powered incentives could be justified on economic grounds, that is, where hierarchical modes of organization could be more efficient than the market, the vagueness of property rights characteristic of the communist economies undermined their advantages. The multitude of different influences exerted on management of state-owned or cooperative enterprises made any sound incentive system for managers unfeasible.[5]

EVOLUTION OF PROPERTY RIGHTS PRIOR TO 1960

Property rights during the period of the command economy in Poland developed through a series of distinct stages. During 1945 to 1954, when the basic structure of the command economy was established, the predominant position of state ownership was also built. In the beginning state ownership was accomplished by nationalization and the expropriation of private property. A strategy of forced capital investment further expanded state ownership. In agriculture, the years 1949 to 1954 were marked by attempts to replace individual farmers with state-controlled cooperatives (*kolhozs*).

The years 1955–1957 brought a partial reversal of the previous course. The strategy of forced collectivization of agriculture was abandoned, and the majority of *kolhozs* were dissolved. The policy toward small private businesses outside agriculture became less hostile, making it possible for many of them to reappear.

During 1958–1980, the property structure of the Polish economy was quite stable, with a slow dwindling of the share of private property due to the prevailing discrimination against this property form.

The limited economic reform of the last phase of the command economy (1981–1989) included some changes in property rights. First, the hostility toward private property was declared unjustified. The change manifested itself in constitutional guarantees to private farmers. Also, private foreign capital was allowed to invest in Poland, although in the beginning this was limited to small investors of Polish origin. As the policy toward private business became more liberal, private firms grew. Their numbers proliferated and their employment almost doubled between 1980 and 1989. As a result, the contribution of the non-agricultural private sector to national income grew from 6.0 percent in 1980 to 9.7 percent in 1989. Many of the present Polish capitalists owe their fortunes to the more favorable business environment created in the 1980s.

The changes in property rights in the 1980s were also expressed in attempts to reform state ownership. There were two critical issues at stake.

It was openly recognized that relations between the management of state-owned enterprises and the commanding ranks of the economy had to be reformed. The 1981 law on state-owned enterprises set explicit limits to the state's control over its enterprises and granted enterprises much broader scope of decisions. Special bodies, called founding organs, were charged with responsibility to supervise state-owned enterprises, replacing the previous multitude of influences.

The other issue pertained to the internal governance structure of state-owned enterprises. Solidarity, which gained some political authority before martial law was imposed in December 1981, supported a revival movement for workers' management.[6] Workers' management was considered by some Solidarity activists as a guarantee that the maze of unrestricted external interventions into enterprise management would not be restored. Others regarded it as a means to "socialize" state ownership and thereby to come closer to the goals of "genuine" socialism.

After a political clash, a compromise, which established legal foundations for workers' management, was reached between Solidarity and communist authorities. A kind of internal diarchy was created. The internal governance of state-owned enterprises was divided between the enterprise director and employees. The powers of employees included some important decision-making rights. They could, through their representatives on employees' councils, participate in the procedure of appointment of the enterprise directors. The employees' councils could audit some managerial decisions of enterprise directors. Employees could also share in profits of their enterprises. These property rights of employees have survived and have even been strengthened in the 1989 amendment to the law on state-owned enterprises.

The governance structure of the state-owned sector that emerged shaped the reforms of the 1980s. Although more explicitly defined than in the past, they were poorly designed and contained many ambiguities. The consequences of this structure have a bearing on present problems of the functioning and transformations of state-owned enterprises.

RECENT DEVELOPMENTS IN PROPERTY RIGHTS

The Beginning of Radical Transformation of the Polish Economy and the Debate on Property Reform

The stunning victory of Solidarity in the parliamentary elections of June 1989 ended the years of communist rule in Poland. The new government, led by Tadeusz Mazowiecki, pledged a transformation of Poland into a Western-style market economy. A radical reform of property rights was proclaimed as a main issue of the transformation. The new government's concern for property reforms manifested itself in the immediate opening of a new Office of the Government Plenipotentiary for Ownership Transformations. Later, the office was converted into the Ministry for Ownership Transformations. The office, and later the ministry, was charged with the task of working out basic tenets of the ownership transformation, preparing the legal framework for it, and training future experts on property reforms.

Working out the strategy for property reforms in the present Polish situation is not an easy task. The difficulties are formidable and the subject matter is extremely complex. It is no wonder that the attempts to work out a strategy of privatization are accompanied by heated debate. Several opposing views can be distinguished in the debate.

According to the less radical view, property reform should be limited to what is called the commercialization of state-owned enterprises, which means transforming state-owned enterprises from quasi-government institutions into company structures operating on commercial lines, though owned by the government. The proponents of this view do not regard privatization as a necessary part of the property reforms, since they assume that it is not property rights that determine the performance of the market economy, but competition. Therefore, they consider the de-monopoliza-tion of the economy much more important than privatization.

Most observers, however, consider privatization one of the main direc-tions for property reforms, although they differ on some critical issues of privatization.

The first issue involves the mode of transferring the state-owned assets into private hands. Here, two views can be distinguished. According to the first view, the assets should be sold at prices set according to expert evaluations or determined by demand and supply. The proponents of this view regard the privatization experience in the West (mainly in Britain) as the model. They argue that only this mode is up to the standards of the market economy and has been proved in practice. Their opponents claim that, due to the shortage of private savings, the flotation of state-owned assets would be slow, while radical and fast privatization is needed to boost the performance of the economy. They propose instead a free distribution of the state-owned assets. This could be accomplished, for instance, by giving away vouchers that could be used only to buy shares of firms being privatized. Opponents of the idea of free distribution of shares of privatized companies say, in turn, that this arrangement would lead to firms having so many owners that no control could be exercised over managers.

The next controversial issue is the scope of preferences afforded to employees of privatized enterprises. Some proponents of employee pref-erences maintain that shares should be given away only to employees. Others, inspired by the development of employee stock ownership plans (ESOPs),[7] propose to help employees to buy shares by supplying them with cheap loans or giving them tax relief. These proposals are criticized as unjust because employees who work for establishments that will not be privatized (schools, post offices, etc.) cannot enjoy these preferences.

Many other disputes exist over the rights to initiate privatization proce-dures, to approve decisions, and to supervise the whole process. Advocates of government control of the process of privatization clash here with those who are for decentralization, that is, for giving the right of initiative to enterprises themselves and for entrusting the procedure to independent (private) bodies.

Another issue is the role of foreign capital in privatization. Here, views extend from an acceptance of free access of foreign capital to defense of the Polish economy against foreign buyouts in any form.

Some of these issues have turned into political controversies. One of the hottest political clashes occurred over the problem of employee preferences. A strong faction in Solidarity, which has its political base in the movement for workers' self-management, forcefully supported ideas of distributing state-owned property to employees on preferential terms. This political group, through vigorous lobbying in the parliament, attempted to impose a bill that would guarantee preferences for employees. However, its gains were modest and only limited preferences were afforded. The idea of free distribution of shares of privatized enterprises to the general public figured in the presidential campaign of Lech Walesa, whose political influence undoubtedly contributed to the endorsement of the idea by the government in the process of working out basic tenets of privatization strategy.

The disparate views outlined above reflect different ideological positions and analytic considerations. Choices or compromises have been necessary in order to work out basic principles of property reforms.

Privatization Strategy of State Industrial Firms

The privatization strategy that has gradually emerged is contained mainly in two important documents. The first is the Law on Privatization passed by the parliament; the other is the Program of Privatization.[8]

There were several reasons that a separate law on privatization had to be passed. The complicated authority structure of the state-owned enterprises required the specification of the decision rights of all of the bodies involved in the privatization procedure.[9] At the same time, the new law defined the basic legal options of privatizing. These options were:

1. Transformation of state-owned enterprises into state-owned corporations and selling their stock to the general public.
2. Liquidation of state-owned enterprises in order to sell them wholly or in part.
3. Leasing state-owned firms, or parts of them, to partnerships with the option to purchase, after some time. (Partnerships of employees are preferred. Only when employees decide not to create a partnership may other partnerships apply.)

According to the law, the initiative to privatize a state-owned enterprise can be taken by organs of the enterprise (its director and employees' council), by its founding organ, or by the Ministry for Ownership Transformations. In each case, the final decision is made by the Ministry for Ownership Transformations. The law also provides some restrictions on acquisition of shares of privatized enterprises by foreign investors. A foreign investor must obtain the approval of the Agency for Foreign Investment if he or she intends to buy more than 10 percent of the shares or wants to buy preferred stock.

While the Law on Privatization creates the needed legal framework, the program outlines privatization policy. It provides for three patterns of privatization.

A limited number of bigger companies will be privatized on a case-by-case basis. This is the "individual" mode. This method will be used for those enterprises that have their own programs of privatization or that can attract foreign investors. The value of such enterprises will be determined by independent consulting firms. Their stock will be offered for sale in the form of public flotation.

The flotation of the first five enterprises started in December 1990 and was accompanied by massive advertising. The subscription for the sale of their stock was closed in the beginning of January 1991.

The second method pertains to about 450 to 500 big, state-owned enterprises that are to be privatized by distributing their stock. Their privatization is to be preceded by corporatization. The corporatization assumes that supervisory councils (one-third of which is employees' representatives and two-thirds are members appointed by the state) will replace the present impractical governance structure.

The rules for distribution of the stock are as follows. Employees of privatized enterprises will receive 10 percent of the stock. The equivalent of 30 percent of the stock will be given away to the general public in the form of "privatization vouchers" and another 30 percent will go to institutional investors. A part of the vouchers (20 percent of the stock) will be earmarked for the Social Security Department (ZUS) to create a fund from which pensions can be financed. Also, state banks will get some part of the vouchers (about 10 percent of the stock), which will be used for their capitalization before they are privatized.

The possessors of the vouchers can use them to buy shares of investment funds, investment banks, or other institutional investments. Institutional investors, in turn, will be allowed to use the vouchers to buy the stock of privatized enterprises at special auctions. This means that only selected institutional investors will directly own the stock of this category of privatized enterprises. This arrangement serves two purposes. First, it reduces the risk to small investors. Second, it provides conditions for effective ownership control over management in situations of dispersion of shares. In addition, only blocks of stock will be sold to selected investors at the auctions in order to further strengthen their control potential. For the same reason, the state will entrust the institutional investors with the remaining 30 percent of the stock.

The distribution of vouchers and the auctions of stock was to start in the second half of 1991. Seventy percent of the stock of 150 to 200 of the large, state-owned enterprises were to be floated in this way by the end of 1991. According to the plan, by the end of 1993, the stock of the biggest 450 to 500 enterprises would be transferred into private hands.

The third pattern of privatization concerns the remaining 5,500 to 6,000 medium-sized and smaller enterprises. They will be privatized in a decentralized way, with the participation of founding organs, regional agencies of the Ministry for Ownership Transformations, and the enterprises themselves. In addition to selling whole enterprises or their assets, this privatization pattern also allows, in some cases, for management contracts to be concluded with individuals or firms, Polish or foreign. Leasing the liquidated firms to partnerships of employees or establishing joint ventures is the next option that can be taken up in this pattern.

The Program of Privatization assumes that in three years, half of the state-owned industrial assets will be privatized, and that in five years the property structure of the Polish economy will be not too different from that of Western European economies.

The privatization of state-owned enterprises is to be accompanied by efforts to create a stock market. This will be a major undertaking that will include: drafting a law on securities, the establishment of a Securities Commission, the training of future brokers, and so on. The Warsaw Stock Exchange, modeled after the Stock Exchange in Lyon, France, was to be initiated in the middle of 1991. (The French model of capital market was recognized as the most appropriate to the Polish economy.)

The privatization of the "hard core" of the state economy is the most challenging part of the Polish property reforms. Although the basic elements of the strategy for this privatization have already been worked out, many questions are still unanswered. The important details concerning issuing the privatization vouchers and their tradeability have not been decided. It is also by no means clear how implementation of the strategy will proceed. The performance of institutional investors seems to be one of the critical issues as well.

"Small-Scale" Privatization

The above-described Program of Privatization does not refer explicitly to the vast sector of economy consisting of small shops, restaurants, barbers, repair shops, and so on. Privatization of these businesses, called "small" privatization, started much earlier and advanced much further by the end of 1990. The small privatization started with the leasing of premises on which the businesses were run. The businesses were freed from administrative controls in the spring of 1990. (The previous controls are one more example of the ways that property rights were attenuated by the state.)

The fast pace of the small privatization does not mean, however, that it is free from problems. The first attempts to invite bids for leasing the premises showed that some businesses could not compete with others. For instance, owners of fashion stores could offer much higher rents than owners of grocery stores or bookstores. Residents of some neighborhoods protested when basic kinds of businesses began disappearing.[10] It was then decided that in some situations, rent control would be applied. Another conflict occurred when employees of shops to be privatized protested to try to protect their jobs. To resolve this conflict, partnerships of employees have been given priority to take over privatized businesses.

In spite of these problems, it seems that small privatization qualifies as a success. Privatized shops and restaurants can be found everywhere, and they offer their clients better service and a greater variety of goods, sometimes at lower prices.

Reform of Cooperative Ownership

As was pointed out earlier, the command economy in Poland subsumed cooperative ownership under state control and made it resemble state ownership. The system of commands and resource allocation were fully implemented in the cooperative sector of ownership. This was institutionalized by establishing a hierarchical organization for cooperatives. Every cooperative had to join a regional union that was, in turn, a compulsory member of a central union. The hierarchy of cooperative organizations served the same purpose as the hierarchical organization of the state sector: central management by means of commands and resource allocations.

The position of cooperative members was reduced to the role of work force (in producer cooperatives) or clients (in other kinds of cooperatives), which meant that their property rights were insignificant. The control bodies (supervisory councils, management boards), though nominally elected by members, in reality were appointed by supreme unions.

It goes without saying that the property reforms aimed at creating appropriate ownership foundations for the market system could not leave out the cooperative sector. The new government was quick to implement the reform of cooperative ownership. In January 1990, an amendment to the Cooperative Law was passed that aimed at restoring genuine cooperative ownership.

The law abolished the hierarchical organization of the cooperative sector by a compulsory dissolution of all cooperative unions. No new unions could be restored until July 1991. In addition, mandatory elections of representatives for supervisory councils were to be held within two months.

The results of the reform are mixed. Cooperatives became truly independent, but the results of the elections were disappointing.[11] The participation of members in the elections was very low, and it seems that in most cooperatives, previous representatives were re-elected. This means, on the one hand, that the representative bodies and governing cooperatives have not become more credible and, on the other, that members of cooperatives generally do not exhibit "ownership spirit" (i.e., active participation in their affairs).

To remedy the situation, some people advocate repeating the elections but preparing for them more adequately this time. This means, among other things, putting more stress on educating and instructing the members of cooperatives.

It has also been pointed out that the present capital structure of most cooperatives undermines the ownership interest of their members. Due to regulations imposed during the former system, the members' shares constitute only a small fraction of cooperatives' capital (most capital coming from undistributed reserves). It is advocated, then, that the members' shares should be revalued. Existing cooperative law does not allow for a clear distinction between the position of members and that of employees who can become members by the very fact of their employment. This is also blamed for undermining ownership interests of cooperative members.

It seems that in many cases, attempts to revitalize cooperative property are doomed to fail, however. Numerous cooperatives do not have sound economic bases. They were created only because government policy toward the cooperative sector was more benign than toward the private sector of ownership. Privatization of part of the cooperatives, by dissolving them or by turning them into partnerships, seems inevitable.

Creation of Municipal Property

Creation of municipal property was one of the means recommended to remedy the ailments of the state leviathan. Local authorities have been regarded as better placed for the management of public land, buildings, or utilities. Therefore, in May 1990, a law was passed that separated municipal ownership from state ownership. At the same time, an administrative reform divided Poland into several thousands of municipalities, and elections for municipal councils were held.

The formal start of municipal property has brought many problems. In part, they can be ascribed to the lack of experience of people ruling municipalities. The new municipal councils do not perform satisfactorily yet. In part, they reflect the difficult choices that confront municipalities now. A typical dilemma would be to decide whether a municipal building should be earmarked for a public library or leased to a private business in order to increase revenue. These problems are quite new because under the old system local expenses were covered by the central government.

Municipal councils also face the problem of privatization of their property. They "inherited" from the state vast possessions of real estate and houses that, in many instances, seem to be more fit for private property. The same condition exists among numerous former state-owned enterprises that have been shifted to municipal control (i.e., municipalities have become their founding organs). It is expected that many of them should now be transferred into private hands.

Strengthening of Private Property Rights and Development of Private Ownership

The last important element of property reforms in Poland has been the strengthening of private property rights.

The economic liberalization implemented in Poland in 1989-1990 brought a great improvement in this respect. The freedom to set prices is almost complete now. Freedom of entrepreneurship (the right to start a business) is also present. The unequal treatment of private ownership as compared with state ownership, so characteristic of the communist system, has been obliterated. For instance, the restraints limiting the size of private firms to no more than fifty employees have been lifted. Amendments have been passed to restore rights of private owners. Previous limits on possession and trade of agricultural land have been abolished. Real estate owners can no longer be dispossessed from their property without appropriate indemnities, and their rights to develop their possessions cannot be curtailed by routine administrative decisions. These examples could be multiplied.

Private owners reacted to the new property environment with vigorous entrepreneurship. In spite of a severe recession caused by the drastic monetary and fiscal measures of the 1990 stabilization program, the number of private firms is growing fast. In the first half of 1990, the number of private firms increased by 6 percent, and the number of private partnerships almost doubled.

CONCLUSION

The property reforms initiated in Poland to build the foundations for a sound market economy are daring. No country has ever attempted a complete transition from an economy whose property structure is dominated by state ownership to an economy based on pluralistic structure of property with predominance of private ownership. Both the scale of the endeavor and the pace of needed reforms make previous experiences of property reforms of limited relevance. Conceptual and implementation problems are paramount.

It took much time, effort, and debate to determine the main directions of the reforms, work out their elementary tenets, and pass basic laws. The blueprint stage for property reforms is not over, however. The policy of property reforms may change under the influence of future events.

Some results of the property reforms that have been implemented are encouraging. Other results highlight problems to overcome and possible modifications. The significance of many threats is still unknown.

NOTES

1. For instance, the general public has never learned who took the decision to construct the gigantic steelworks Katowice, for which the economic rationale is very doubtful and the environmental consequences are disastrous.

2. This endeavor was particularly evident during the Stalinist period (1948–1954). Later, the ambitions of communist authorities to impose a totalitarian dictatorship gradually dwindled. In the last period of communist rule, there were not even attempts to provide any ideological justification.

3. Poland was often accused by Soviet ideologues of lagging behind other socialist countries because of the prevailing strong private sector in agriculture.

4. The consequences of various property arrangements are studied by property rights theory. According to this theory, non-private property rights are non-exclusive and non-transferable. These attributes result in difficulties of internalizing external effects, which in turn undermine and distort incentives of economic actors. A recent exposition of the property rights theory can be found in Barzel (1990).

5. The distinction between the high-powered incentives of the market and low-powered incentives of hierarchies has been made by Oliver Williamson (Williamson 1985: Chap. 6), who has discussed the economic logic on which these two kinds of incentives are based. According to Williamson, different kinds of incentives fit into different economic situations. High-powered incentives are not a workable arrangement in hierarchical organizations.

6. The idea of workers' management gained some popularity after political changes in 1956, which marked the end of the Stalinist era, but was quickly

suppressed by the ruling communists, who feared that the idea could be used to undermine the centralized management of the economy.

7. Information on ESOPs can be found, for example, in Rosen, Klein, and Young (1985).

8. The government led by Tadeusz Mazowiecki managed to release the program just before his resignation in November 1990. The new prime minister, Jan K. Bielecki, has already announced that some corrections to the program will be needed.

9. The authority structure got even more complicated when the Ministry for Ownership Transformations was created.

10. This situation reflects the acute shortage of premises. Due to specific properties of the command economy in Poland, too few new premises have been built.

11. However, some critics point out that the forced liquidation of all unions left the primary cooperatives without any support services (e.g., management advice and audit service), which cooperatives in market economies receive from their unions.

Chapter 4

Transition into a Market Economy: The Road to Privatization in Yugoslavia

Ivan Ribnikar

It is not worthwhile to criticize monetary policy (or "monetary-credit" policy, as it has been wrongly and characteristically called in Yugoslavia), interest rate policy, exchange-rate policy or macroeconomic policy in general,[1] because the basic problems of the Yugoslav economy lie in the most fundamental characteristics of this third economic system, the so-called market-planned economic system. A transition into a market economy cannot be achieved only or mainly through changes in the conduct of the economic policy. Putting too much emphasis on the conduct of the economic policy misses the point. By focusing on economic policy, unwillingly or with good intentions, grave mistakes could be made, and the conclusion could be quite wrong. Economic policy, from the standpoint of the market economy, had to be wrong, strong, or peculiar to enable business enterprises to keep producing goods in the market-planned economy. Only such an economic policy could somehow (the details of which shall be explained in this chapter) neutralize the peculiarities of the third economic system and make economic life look, at least on the surface, approximately normal.

An adequate path for the transition from the market-planned into the market economy cannot be found without precise knowledge of the essential features, functioning, and residual aspects of the market-planned economy. In the first three sections of this chapter, we shall present this necessary background information on the Yugoslav market-planned system. In the fourth section, a desirable transition will be explained, with particular emphasis on the introduction of the private ownership of business enterprises as the centerpiece of a market economy. Suggestions are given on how to proceed with the introduction of ownership of business enterprises. In the final section, some very brief remarks are made on what is to be expected in Yugoslavia. The desired logical path should not be expected if the changes made so far are any guide to future changes.

BASIC CHARACTERISTICS OF THE MARKET-PLANNED ECONOMY

The departure from the centrally planned economy in Yugoslavia started in the beginning of the 1950s. This was very early, as compared with other neighboring countries. The dominant idea at that time was that the new economic system should no longer be centrally planned, but that at the same time it should not be simply a market economy. A market economy meant capitalism, which was the ideology of the establishment.[2]

We Yugoslavs were lucky enough to start phasing out a centrally planned economy early on, but we were caught in the trap of a third economic system (neither centrally planned nor market), something nonexistent up to that time, something very dimly conceived, burdened with utopian ideas and something that was not supposed to change or undermine the existing power structure, that is, the leading role of the Communist Party. Nevertheless, the majority of Yugoslav economists were attracted to exploring the new world.[3] They were proud to be among the vanguards of a new system. We must admit that *tertium non datur* was not accepted and that they were supported even by some Western economists—those outside the mainstream.

From the beginning of the 1950s until the end of the 1980s, numerous changes in the economic system were made—usually designed as reforms and proclaimed by the establishment as revolutionary changes. However, the basic characteristics of the economic system remained unchanged. Putting aside the paraphernalia, we can see three dominant features of the system: social ownership of business enterprises, workers' self-management, and, neglected by all, peculiar finance, which I called "cranky" finance.[4]

Social ownership means that the permanent funds of business enterprises are not owned by any natural or legal person. They are "owned" by and belong to the society, which is something unidentifiable. This concept is elucidated by looking at the balance sheet of a typical enterprise in Figure 4.1. We can say that social ownership is defined negatively: No natural or legal person is allowed to be the owner. In the past, business enterprises, whatever their name (until recently they were called "organi-

Figure 4.1
Balance Sheet of Business Enterprise in the Market-Planned Economy

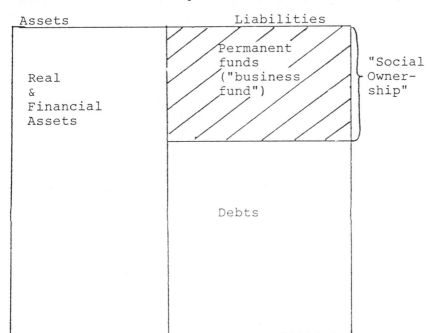

zations of associated labor"), were legal entities and, as such, owners of all their assets.

Workers' self-management[5] means that workers should have the same role (in addition to being workers, of course) as shareholders in joint stock companies, even though they are not owners of the company, are not entitled to dividends, and cannot sell the business enterprise. There is no appropriate division between workers and managers. In Yugoslavia, managers are workers and they are members of the trade union and, in the majority of cases, of the Communist Party.

Social ownership of business enterprises goes together with workers' self-management. Both characteristics are very attractive, and, as such, very dangerous.

If one looks at the third characteristic, the financing of the system, one comes to the conclusion that the system is utopian. Two problems appear. The first is how a new business enterprise starts. Who will provide capital or permanent funds? Can they be found? They should have the following characteristics: they should have money to spend for whatever purposes they wish, but they should decide to invest it permanently into a new business enterprise, although they know in advance that their investment will be transformed into social property, that they will lose their money, and that they will have no say in the business enterprise started with their capital. It means that altruists are needed; but as soon as one comes across an altruist, one may be sure that he is leaving economics and entering a utopian world.

The second financing problem concerns the expansion of existing business enterprises. Who should provide permanent funds in excess of retained earnings or undistributed profits, especially if they are non-existent? Moreover, because of huge interest payments and repayments of debt, there is no cash flow to be expected. The answer is the same: Altruists are needed.

Thus, the market-planned economic system is illogical and inconsistent. It is not even possible as a model: tertium non datur. Nevertheless, the system has been functioning somehow in Yugoslavia since the beginning of the 1950s. It has been economically more efficient than the centrally planned economies and, until the beginning of the 1980s, it was in some respects (permanence of employment, non-competitive environment, free and extensive social services) more pleasant than a number of market economies. The latter was possible only, as will be seen, by permanently transferring costs to the future (via foreign indebtedness, increases in the hidden public debt, and disinvestment of the long-lived fixed capital). Until the beginning of the 1980s, the criticisms just presented would have been ridiculed. But we first must explain the functioning of this system, which should have not existed at all.

FUNCTIONING OF THE SYSTEM

If we put aside the strange idea (though postulated even by prestigious economists) that a business enterprise can start up only with credits and can stay with such a financial structure as a going concern indefinitely, one of the peculiarities of these newly started business enterprises in Yugoslavia was, nevertheless, great indebtedness. Moreover, very small amounts of permanent funds were required despite their significant indebtedness.

The permanent funds were not provided by altruists, but by the Communist Party, the government—by those who were in power. The money provided was not theirs, but that of other enterprises, which were socially owned, governmental, or semi-governmental institutions. At the same time, banks were ordered to give credit. Thus, a business enterprise could start, heavily indebted as it was, and usually with a wrong production line, using quite inadequate technology, and with costs that were too high. The firms had no competition; they played the role of a *deus ex machina*.

But it was not enough for the functioning of the system that deus ex machina had been found. Business enterprises were highly leveraged; the same applied to the expanding, already existing, business enterprises. In normal, non-inflationary surroundings in circumstances of *pacta sunt servanda*, such highly leveraged business enterprises would not be able to survive. Their debt to quasi-equity, permanent funds ("business funds") ratio was, for instance, ten to one or even higher, and their debt was predominantly of a short-term or medium-term nature, to be repaid in installments. The cash flow was generally not sufficient to enable business enterprises to pay interest on their loans.

What was needed in addition to a deus ex machina was an inflationary milieu. Such a milieu would allow business enterprises to raise prices and increase their cash flow, which would enable them to pay interest and keep repaying their debts, but only if nominal interest rates remained unchanged. And they were unchanged until the mid-1980s. Thus, the second problem was solved via inflation, which made interest rates negative in real terms, and which, in effect, turned a large segment of their loans into grants. Inflation was generously tolerated by those in power for other reasons, as they were not aware of the financing function provided by such inflation. It enabled highly indebted business enterprises to survive. What was happening could be explained as "permanent primary accumulation of 'social' capital."[6]

Very soon after, the financial structure of business enterprises, provided they were not an extremely bad investment, started to improve—the debt to permanent funds ratio started to decrease—not as a consequence of undistributed profits, but as a consequence of the depreciation of debt. Wealth was transferred, via banks, from bank creditors (households or individuals) to highly indebted business enterprises. This process was so efficient that the financial structure of business enterprises, usually a few years after their start-up or after major investments in real (usually fixed) assets had been made, was more or less the same as that of business enterprises in market economies—if we treat "business funds" as "equity." In many cases, Yugoslav business enterprises are much less indebted than even business enterprises in market economies.

The market-planned economy required permanent interference of those in power in the affairs of business enterprises. They provided the start-up capital and made banks give business enterprises so much credit that they became, in comparison with firms in market economies, highly indebted. Moreover, there was the generosity of those in power to sustain inflation and thus provide negative real interest rates. As neither of these characteristics is within the realm of rational economics, the uniqueness of the Yugoslav economy is not proof that there is a third way. On the contrary, it is proof that there is no third way. As we shall see, there is, in fact, only one way—or a variety of ways, if we do not look only at the skeleton of market economies but take into account the details of such economies as well.[7]

CONSEQUENCES OF THE RESIDUAL EFFECTS OF THE MARKET-PLANNED ECONOMY

Workers' self-management, or the absence of owners of business enterprises or capitalists, was possible only under three conditions: social ownership, permanent interference of those in power in the affairs of business enterprises and banks, and inflation. The interference of those in power was necessary for two reasons: to provide at least a small amount of permanent funds and to make banks give business enterprises large credits—in many cases ten to twenty times as great as are allowed in market economies. The inflationary milieu was provided by permissive economic policy, in particular by loose monetary policy. The velocity of money was so elastic that it was not necessary that monetary policy be always expansionary.[8] Taking everything into account, there was not genuine workers' self-management. Rather, the control over business enterprises was de facto in the hands of those in power both outside and inside business enterprises. They played the role of capitalists.

For the functioning of such an economy, finance played a crucial role. The basic requirement was a permanent redistribution of wealth to business enterprises, which could not be done other than through negative real interest rates (even if we put aside protection from foreign competition through tariff walls, privileged access to foreign exchanges, etc.). We cannot understand Yugoslav finance without keeping this requirement in mind. One must not be surprised that finances were quite specific—unusual, "cranky" finance.

Redistribution of wealth via banks left them unhurt as long as they gave credits on the basis of deposits denominated in dinars. As individuals learned that they were losing their wealth if they kept it in the form of bank deposits, the propensity to keep savings in banks started to decrease. In the mid-1960s, deposits denominated in foreign currencies (predominantly in German marks) were introduced to diminish the ex-ante gap between investments and savings. As banks continued giving credits denominated in dinars, liabilities of banks started to increase relative to their assets that were denominated in dinars. Due to inflation, the dinar was devalued from time to time, and after the introduction of the fluctuating exchange rate, the dinar depreciated against foreign currencies more or less in accordance with the inflation rate. Once the hard currency reserves, which provided additional savings, were exhausted sometime in the mid-1970s, banks, the National Bank of Yugoslavia (NBY), and business enterprises started to look for capital abroad. They succeeded in getting it. A new kind of liability in foreign denominations appeared on the balance sheets of banks, the NBY and business enterprises—namely, foreign indebtedness.

Banks did not or could not acknowledge the diminishing value of assets as costs to be covered by revenue. They could have done so only by introducing a positive real interest rate on their credits, which was impossible. The economic system would have to come to an end, as there would have been no investment and no new business enterprises.

Genuine losses due to foreign exchange exposure began to increase on the asset side of the banks' balance sheets under the title "other assets" and, later, as "negative foreign exchange differences." When, in the beginning of the 1980s, they became so big that banks could not any longer pretend not to be insolvent (their earning assets shrank substantially), to avoid coming face to face with the true characteristic of the market-planned economic system, the NBY took over almost all "negative foreign exchange differences" from banks and replaced them by claims on the National Bank itself. These "black holes" disappeared from the balance sheets of banks but reappeared on the balance sheets of the NBY. From that moment on, losses at the level of the NBY started to increase. As the NBY is an institution without capital, those losses should have been taken over by the founder of the NBY, the federal government. As this did not happen, increasing "black holes" on the asset side of the NBY balance sheet were debts waiting to be acknowledged by the government. Finally, when the black hole almost covered the whole asset side of the NBY balance sheet, the government acknowledged it as its own debt and started to pay interest on that debt.[9]

But the asset side of commercial banks' balance sheets was not cleaned up when "negative foreign exchange differences" were taken over by the NBY. Large bad loans of a different kind remained. Business enterprises were able to start up or expand only on the basis of enormous bank credits. As the "owners" of banks were business enterprises, their primary goal was to extend large credits under favorable conditions to themselves. The biggest and, at times, the worst business enterprises had the most power, which was usually strengthened by interference from a part of the government, politicians, or the Communist Party. Thus they were beneficiaries of the most sizable credits.

When the system came to its end in the mid-1980s, as the influx of foreign capital ceased and the capital required for growth could no longer be provided by inflation and forced savings, the hangovers of the market-planned economy appeared, that is, big black holes on the asset side of the NBY balance sheet. These black holes represented bad loans on the asset side of commercial banks' balance sheets. They reflected business enter-prises with not so much outdated technology, but with their book values or values at the level of replacement costs, which had very little correspon-dence with their "prospective value" or value at the level of "discounted cash flow." The system could function only within a specific financial system, and the peculiarities of the financial system left the NBY, com-mercial banks, and business enterprises in a ruinous financial shape.

We can identify the end of the system as the point at which it could neither provide growth nor maintain the achieved level of production by transferring costs of its functioning to the future. The future became today. Instead of a net inflow of foreign capital, there was a net outflow, as forced savings were exhausted and it was impossible for long-lived fixed assets to be further depreciated. The end of the market-planned economy came about for economic reasons.[10]

TRANSITION INTO A MARKET ECONOMY

The analysis just provided of the market-planned economy, its function-ing, performance, and hangovers, points to the same conclusion. All three characteristics of the market-planned economy have to be abolished for the simple reason that, despite the attraction of social ownership and workers' self-management, finance does not allow such an economy. Business enterprises should be able to start up and expand without the need for a deus ex machina, and the natural habitat of business enterprises should not be inflation. These are the basic requirements of an efficient economy. An economy cannot be efficient if it does not rely primarily on self-interest and if prices in general (and this includes interest rates) are not market prices.

Once we have in mind this basic financial requirement, everything falls into place. Ownership of business enterprises should be introduced and the owner of business enterprises may be any natural or legal person but not a society, as a society is not a legal person. As soon as there are owners, there is no place for workers' self-management. As the linchpin of eco-nomics, how business enterprises are financed depends on ownership; the problem of transition into a market economy is primarily the problem of ownership.

One form of ownership to be introduced is clear and simple: public or state ownership of business enterprises in industries with natural monopolies (railways, postal services, public utilities, etc.).[11] Once the value of business funds of those social business enterprises to be transformed into genuine public ownership has been determined (as net assets value or discounted expected cash flow value), they are turned into equity capital belonging to the state.

But the majority of business funds of social business enterprises, approximately 70 to 80 percent, cannot be transformed that simply. Ideas abound on how to solve the problem. Let us just mention some of them: (1) All social business enterprises should be nationalized and then immediately privatized—sold to the highest bidders; (2) titles to wealth represented by business funds of social business enterprises should be distributed among workers employed in particular business enterprises (so social business enterprises are transformed into joint stock companies owned by workers); (3) social business enterprises should be transformed into collective ownership by workers employed in particular business enterprises, or business funds of social business enterprises should become the declared property of a business enterprise (it is a "circulus vitiosus" or "incestuous ownership" not known in market economies); and (4) some combination of privatization, distribution and/or collective ownership, or some subvarieties of all of them.

Before we put forward our idea on the solution to the problem of transition, it is important to remind the reader that any approach must start from (or take into account) history, the institutional conditions, the state of mind of the population, and the state of mind of those in power. Owners must be found for such a large amount of wealth that talking about privatization (although in some cases, privatization is the right solution) is nothing but talking nonsense. Efficiency of business enterprises must improve quickly; otherwise, a major part of wealth will be lost. At the same time, the solution to the problem must be fair and accepted by the population as just. It must also be an economically correct solution. Finally, one must keep in mind that, since the beginning of the 1950s, workers were forced to be managers or controllers of business enterprises, and that turned into something quite different. The function of "capitalists" was taken over by politicians. One should be cautious not to force workers this time to become shareholders against their will. Even professionals have very little or no knowledge about shares, capital markets, or finance.

Ownership of business enterprises would be taken over by a small group of people who will become *nouveau riche.*

As social business enterprises are in a difficult state with their indebtedness and/or the amount of permanent fund ("business fund") at their disposal, the timing of their transition into business enterprises should depend on their level of technology and, primarily, their economic performance. The complete transformation of all social business enterprises into business enterprises should be extended over a fairly long period of time. Only in this way can owners of business enterprises be found in the first place on the basis of ability to provide additional input of capital into social business enterprises, can knowledge be acquired, can more knowledgeable managers evolve, and can controlling institutions with the capability to prevent fraud and misuse of financial instruments, such as corporate bonds and shares, be firmly established.

But in order to know how social business enterprises are performing so that they can be transformed at the right moment, their business funds should be declared the property of an institution, such as the "republican" pension fund, which is entitled to fixed dividends but without voting rights, as long as social business enterprises are paying the required dividend to the pension fund.[12] As there is in many cases a substantial difference between the book value and the true value (net assets value or value in the amount of discounted expected cash flow), in a rather short period of time, the value of permanent funds of social business enterprises, under the ownership of pension funds and under obligation to pay dividends, must be assessed.[13]

Under these conditions, the transformation of social business enterprises into business enterprises, or a market-planned economy into a market economy, would follow an optimal path. Workers would not be coerced to become shareholders. Accumulated wealth, created by the process of "permanent primary accumulation of social capital" would be under the ownership of pension funds and remain, in a way, "socialized"; financial instruments such as corporate bonds and shares would not be compromised; and social business enterprises that did not perform well would be forced to change into business enterprises. Ownership of business enterprises would be created predominantly on the basis of additional inflow of capital into the business enterprise. Owners of business enterprises would be workers, other individuals, other business enterprises, banks, and so on. In due time, yet to be determined, all social business enterprises would be transformed into business enterprises. The amount of equity that did not belong to the pension fund (which would remain without voting rights as long as a business enterprise performs well) would become greater than the equity belonging to the pension fund, and after a longer period of time, the ownership of pension funds would become negligible unless pension funds became dominant institutional investors.

Within this general framework, the transformation into business enterprises would rely on the ingenuity, ideas, and imaginations of individuals, and not on the goodness and fairness of the government or of politicians. Within such a framework it would be possible to exploit as far as possible one of the characteristics of the Yugoslav society and economy—the decentralized decision making, the tradition of individuals to rely on themselves and not on a higher authority. The transformation would be performed at an adequate speed and would be correct from an economic point of view. Moreover, the people would accept it as right and fair.

WHAT IS TO BE EXPECTED?

Although it seemed at first that social ownership and workers' self-management would be abandoned with great difficulty because they were home-grown, the process may be slightly different. But it does not mean that the best path, combining adequate speed (from the economic point of view) and changes within the realm of fairness, will be followed. Indoctrination with social ownership and workers' self-management will manifest itself in a variety of ways—some of them strange and unexpected.

Changes are taking place in an environment of depression, of increasing numbers of bankruptcies, and of increased unemployment, which is the consequence of a poorly designed anti-inflationary policy. Such an environment prevents us from choosing the right path because ideas for radical changes are becoming stronger. Ideas to nationalize all business enterprises at once and then to sell them to foreigners and residents or to distribute all "social capital" to workers or individual business enterprises may be accepted as appropriate solutions.

However, the federal government is passing laws on "social capital" that are a curious mixture of Bolshevik activism, radical liberalism, and Vanekism or workers' self management. The first law on social capital was very dangerous.[14] The second law on social capital introduced a curious, roundabout process of transformation of socially owned business enterprises into joint stock companies of mixed ownership on the basis of the so-called internal shares, issued predominantly to workers and others at discounts ranging from 30 to 70 percent.

The number of shares an individual can buy at a discount depends on his or her wages (the maximum amount is three years' wages), and the discount depends on the number of years of employment in the business enterprise. In addition to the 30 percent discount given to all, those employed in the business enterprise have an additional discount of 1 percent for each year of employment up to a maximum total discount of 70 percent.[15] The value of social capital, the basis on which internal shares are to be issued, is to be taken at book value, and shares can be bought on installment payments, up to ten years. Paying for shares is distinct from buying them, because those who have bought shares can stop paying for them if they no longer want to have them. When workers buy shares, and until they pay for them, they get, in reality, something like a "naked warrant" for merits, for years spent in the business enterprise and for the amount of their wages. Internal shares cannot be traded on the financial market.

If we take a look at joint stock companies of mixed ownership on the basis of internal shares we must say that the period of "cranky" finance is not over. Moreover, the door is open for primitive accumulation of capital or for a special variety of an "enfranchisement process."[16] The principle of fairness is not going to be taken into account.

The existing law on social capital is probably not the final word, as the republics will add something with a different flavor. The transition into a market economy is not at hand. Those in power, the old guard or the newcomers, will continue to rely on foreign experts for general ideas or philosophy because they are looking for scientific or expert confirmation of their own prejudices, defunct ideas, and wishful thinking. They will continue to accept their advice (for instance, to nationalize everything and then to sell everything, or to return everything to former owners if they can be found) instead of the preferred way of consulting foreigners on technical matters, avoiding continuation of "cranky" finance, and choosing a transition according to the peculiarities of the market-planned economy as it has functioned so far. We can predict only one thing: The transition will not be as it could or should be.

PRIVATIZATION THAT WE SHOULD AND COULD AFFORD

Privatization of social capital is not possible because the amount of capital that could be privatized is only marginal.[17] This, however, does not mean that we are destined to live with social property and social capital permanently.

Two methods make it possible for us to rid ourselves of these two elements and, thus, also of the planned-market economic system as well. The first method is to distribute the wealth hidden under social capital among citizens—to each the same portion.[18] The second method is to privatize the increase in capital or the increase in the permanent sources of funds of companies by preventing any further increase in social capital.

Preventing any further increase in social capital is in fact a necessity, which cannot be said about the distribution of social capital. Until a genuine financial market is established, citizens should not get shares of individual companies but only shares of an investment company.[19] Individual ownership of business enterprise should initially be possible only through the additional inflow of private capital. Distribution of the existing capital—created on the basis of social capital—should be at least postponed for a few years.

We have only one method left to explain—that based on the prevention of further increase in social capital. Halting further growth of social capital means that the return on it must flow out of those companies. If it flows out of companies, it must flow somewhere. It can only flow to the owner, and for this reason, social capital that is turned into capital does need an owner. This means that social capital is turned into capital once its value is set prospectively, as the value of capital is always determined.

At the moment we are not interested in identifying the actual owner. What is important is that the owner possesses the required attributes. He is not expected to permanently invest the return on his capital into companies. This is the first requirement. Next, he has to agree to limitations on his authority as an owner, which means that he does not possess the right to control companies that he owns solely or partially, providing companies pay him the agreed dividend. It is expected that the company will eventually become a joint stock company, and his share will be shown by preference shares. He will have the right to intervene only if the company temporarily fails to pay the agreed dividend. He could further have a voice in the company if a statutory change of the company were in question, in the event of a company takeover by foreigners, and so on.

The cessation of further growth of social capital is not possible unless it is transformed into public capital (E_j). This is the only feasible way to privatization in this country. A company should open up to the inflow of private capital, and through this inflow, control of the company will pass into the hands of private owners (domestic or foreign, natural and legal persons). We will only be able to refer to the openness of companies if a balance between the advantages that private owners expect from their permanent investments in companies (control and expected return) and the disadvantages (the burden of a loss that might occur) is established and continuously maintained at the adequate level, if savings of private sector are turned into equity (E_z).

The owner of companies, who has become an owner on the basis of capital that has been transformed from social capital (E_j), is not an appropriate owner if he is satisfied with the dividend received. He must ensure a situation in which companies are constantly open to the inflow of extra capital. This is what makes privatization a regular and long-term process, lasting as long as permanent sources of funds grow (or until the onset of a new social revolution that will once again abolish private property).

Since this is to be a regular process, we must first learn what profit or loss a company may have. We must set up a system to provide legally required information, which will make rational economic decision making possible. Since we are dealing with capital (E), we need information that will tell us whether capital in a certain physical form should grow and by what amount, remain at the same level, or decrease and by what amount.

The framework of this continuous process allows for genuine privatization of what has been transformed from social capital into public capital (E_j). At some remote time, when the financial market is established, it may also become possible to distribute equally among citizens the capital that now belongs to us jointly. Nevertheless, it will probably become evident in the future that neither distribution nor privatization of social capital would be economically or socially desirable or opportune.

Thus, a simple and direct transition to a market economy with ownership and capital could be feasible. However, this does not mean that we shall step into a world without problems. We shall enter a world with common and normal problems, the problems that any market economy faces.

But for the success of the process, it is extremely important that a balance is maintained as we have already discussed, and that wealth whose growth is based on savings finds its way to companies in the form of permanent investment. Let us examine how such a balance could be established and maintained.

As long as companies do not possess any private capital (E_z), and provided they pay the agreed and determined dividend on the capital which has been transformed from "social capital" (E_j), any eventual profit is distributed among employees, management, and the owner of the capital according to a preset ratio. It should be arranged so that the amount of extra profit that goes to the employees and management is dependent on the amount of non-private capital per employee. The smaller the amount of non-private capital a company possesses, the greater the amount of extra profit available for distribution. On the one hand, we would thus be able to avoid the apparently insoluble problem of setting the dividend on preference shares that belong to the owner and, through him, to all the citizens. This would bring us to participating preference shares, under which employees and company management are entitled to participation in profits that exceed the amount of the preset value of the dividend. On the other hand, the introduction of the system would ensure that the maximization of profits was itself in the interest of the employees and management alike.[20]

Since the period with no private capital (E_z) is only temporary, the openness of companies should be ensured. However, this can only be done if the balance between what is in the interest of investors and what seems to be a burden to them is established, while an appropriate inflow of capital (E_z) into companies in the form of permanent investment is maintained. Let us examine first the method of distribution of profit between private (E_z) and non-private or public capital (E_j).

Preference shares are issued according to the amount of public capital obtained from social capital. As it is difficult to set the dividend for such a preference share, since it should be neither too low nor too high and error in both directions is possible, we try to avoid the problem as we have avoided it in companies with no private capital. Not all the shares should be declared participating, for fear that an owner of private capital might expect only as high a return as a public owner might expect on its capital. This amount would not be attractive enough to a private investor. Only part of the total shares could be declared participating. What we might try to achieve is that in companies with private capital (E_z) of up to 25 percent of all company capital, the same amount of public capital is transformed into non-participating preference shares (E_{jp}). Figure 4.2 represents a possible situation.

If this were the case, the dividend per preference share could be set at 2 or 3 percent. The surplus profit should, after 3 percent per preference share has been paid, pay out 3 percent per ordinary share held by individuals. Eventual surplus profit, after the 3 percent dividend per ordinary share has been paid out, is distributed proportionally among ordinary shares, and only among those preference shares that are participating.

If we examine a fictional example, we can see whether the system would appeal to individuals. We ignore here a very decisive factor in permanent investment into companies: the loss factor, or the burden of loss. Let us assume there are 20 monetary units of private capital, which constitute 20 percent of all capital, and 80 monetary units, which constitute 80 percent of public capital. Profit amounts to 20 monetary units, or 20 percent with regard to all capital $(E = E_j + E_z = 100)$. Preference shares earn the first 3 percent, that is, 2.4 monetary units of profit. Next, the same sum that pays

Figure 4.2
The Changing Structure of Preference Shares (participating versus non-participating in Relation to the Share of Private Capital (E_z) in All Company Capital (E))

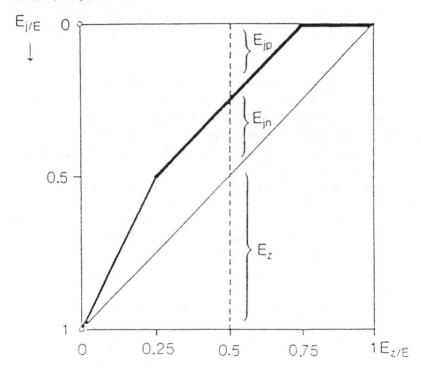

a dividend also enters private capital, that is, 0.6 of a monetary unit. The remaining profit, 17 monetary units, is distributed to 80 percent of capital (to E_z and E_{jp}). Private capital earns a quarter of the profit, that is, 4.25 monetary units, and public capital earns three-quarters, or 12.75 monetary units. The total that goes to private capital is 4.85 monetary units of profit. Its return is 24.25 percent, while public capital earns 15.15 monetary units of profit, which indicates that the value of a dividend is 18.9 percent. The average return on this capital is 20 percent.

The attraction to private investors is not secured only by the expected return on their capital (in addition to the control to which they are entitled as long as they pay the agreed dividend per preference share), but also by spreading the risk of loss. If the total share of private capital (E_z/E) is small, a private investor will not invest capital for fear of a loss. Since it has been anticipated that only part of the preference shares can be held by a public, non-participating share owner, the same principle should be applied to spreading the burden of a loss. In line with this principle, the loss (either current or at the time of liquidation of a company) would be shared proportionally between private capital (E_z) and the portion of public capital that is in the form of participating preference shares (E_{jp}). In our case, the loss would be shared in a ratio of one to three. We could set up another arrangement, but the decisive factor is whether private owners find it attractive enough to invest their capital permanently in companies with only, or predominantly, public capital.

The mechanism described, or variants of it, may begin the only method of privatization feasible in this country, time-consuming though it is. While this process, which will be extremely long, is ongoing, the door to privatization of capital transformed from social capital (E_j) through its sale to residents and foreigners will be kept open. Thus, the kind of privatization that we could and should afford will not prevent privatization of former social capital. When the financial market is established, it will be possible to distribute part or all of the capital, which is identified as E_j, among citizens. (At the same time, it might be possible to give former owners compensation for nationalization, which was de facto confiscation, in a form that everybody dreads now—a form that, everywhere else, is favored and found attractive.) It is of utmost importance that at the very beginning of privatization we have companies, capital, ownership, and owners, that we know how to distinguish between management and employees, and that we are at the same time able to articulate the interest of all those concerned (employees, management, and owners).

Otherwise, as foreseen by the Slovene or any other law on privatization, nationalization and rumors about privatization will be trapped by a more or less inadequate legal language. Privatization that we can and should afford immediately creates an appropriate framework, and within this framework there is enough room for privatization of former social capital, for its distribution among citizens, and for compensation to those who have been deprived in various ways. We must not delay the process of privatization, for it spells normalization of the economy and the society, which ought to have occurred two years ago.

Finally, I would like to say a few words about the owner of the public capital, identified as E_j. This owner can be anyone who possesses those essential characteristics that we have described, and who uses the income earned in the form of dividends per preference share (participating and non-participating) for purposes that recognize that the reality behind this concept of property is the whole body of citizens. (In some distant future we might even decide to distribute the capital among ourselves.[21]) The capital earned should not be invested permanently in a company that is not and will not be state owned, because these companies should remain open to private capital, or to the process of privatization, which is now about to begin and will continue indefinitely. Such an owner can be a pension fund, although, despite the beliefs of many experts and politicians, this is not the only form in which the essence of privatization can be embodied. This essence lies elsewhere, in something these experts and politicians are incapable of seeing.

NOTES

1. By analyzing the monetary system and monetary policy, we were unveiling the very strange world of the market-planned economy. At the beginning of the 1980s, we exhausted this topic and moved through our research to the very basis of the system—to the financing of business enterprises—and through this process, we came to the topic of ownership.

2. We will not talk about "capitalism," an expression burdened with ideology and prejudices, but about the market economy. Although "capitalism" was invented by Marx, those who claim not to be Marxists prefer "capitalism" to "market economy."

3. Some of them were probably advocating workers' self-management in the market-planned economy, as the only alternative to it at that time was a centrally planned economy.

4. As noted by Hansen (1949: 18), monetary cranks were always around and their presence in Yugoslavia was no exception. But there was a difference. In Yugoslavia, monetary and, we must add, financial cranks were within the establishment, responsible for the "theoretical" foundations of the market-planned economic system.

5. It should be called workers' self-control or control. The word *samoupravljanje* has been wrongly translated. It has been acknowledged, more or less, from the beginning that specific knowledge is required for managing business enterprises, although no clear division between workers and managers has been made.

6. See Ribnikar (1989: 57).

7. The study of comparative economic systems will not disappear. It will become more historical, institutional, and finely tuned as the basic characteristics of different societies will be more or less the same everywhere.

8. One of the peculiarities of the functioning of the Yugoslav economy has been the recurring problem of illiquidity of business enterprises. This meant, in the first place, that because of inadequate expansionary or accommodating monetary policy, money has been moving away from business enterprises toward non-business sectors, where no money substitutes were available. Business enterprises could survive by not paying bills to other business enterprises. The accumulation of trade credits and decrease in the proportion of money in the business sector has been called illiquidity.

9. All measures taken by the government had one sole purpose: to enable the economic system to keep going. The government was not prepared to admit that there was something very wrong in the depths of the system.

10. Nevertheless, a transition into the market economy can be extended over a longer period of time. Not all business enterprises are in the same bad position. Some of them may stay as they are for quite a long period if the economic policy is the right one.

11. It does not mean that they will remain so indefinitely. They may be privatized sometime in the future but, for the time being, they may stay publicly owned.

12. It is very important to stop further increases of social capital because it will put pressure on business enterprises to open up, that is, to try to get genuine capital. The only way to do it is to make business enterprises pay dividends on social capital, for example, to the republican pension fund.

13. Those in power either do not understand (or do not want to understand) the point, or they feel a bit uneasy advocating ownership of pension funds, as they may be already quite ripe for retirement. A pension fund for those who want to look "macho" is not how they need to promote themselves.

14. If the law remained unchanged and business conditions continued to deteriorate, business enterprises in social ownership would start to be transferred into the hands of foreigners and residents at bargain prices. By an inappropriate law, the government tremendously increased the risk for investors.

15. Those employed outside the business sector are treated according to the Stalinist dogma as unproductive and, as such, are excluded from this additional discount above 30 percent.

16. As found in Poland and Hungary and criticized by many, such as Polish economist Winiecki ("Enter Comrade Capitalist" 1989: 36).

17. Citizens do not have adequate assets to trade for the shares of business enterprises being privatized. The only available and adequate assets are "foreign exchange deposits," foreign money "under the mattress," and savings abroad. But these assets are probably not greater than 10 percent of the value of social capital to be privatized.

18. The distribution among employees of various companies cannot be taken seriously, though some people may get rich by selling algorithms, which facilitate the exact calculation of any individual or collective contribution to the social capital of a company. The discovery of the algorithm may be seen as a great complement to the planned economic system.

19. Because in this way citizens would become indirect owners of companies (only the investment fund would stand between them and the companies), the same situation might be reached by simply finding an owner who would ensure and establish a form of ownership representing all citizens (i.e., to each the same portion).

20. The problem of appointing and confirming the management of companies in which there is no private owner (the owner is an absentee or passive owner) must be solved in a way that allows for the fact that E_j represents

property owned by all citizens (to each the same portion), property which, in the long run, might be distributed among citizens.

21. In our example, there is no mention of selling social capital at a discount. If such a sale is in question, there are two incompatible points to be considered, namely, the distribution of gifts and the sale of social capital. The theory is based on the demagogic notion that working people should not be disappointed in their expectations, although the same concern applies when selling social capital on "hire purchase." Citizens, and among them those who are employed elsewhere, are looking for something entirely different, something they cannot expect from legislation, and, above all, not from the Law on Privatization.

Part II

Macroeconomic Issues

The Unexpected Consequences of Traditional Macro Stabilization Policy During Transition: The Case of Poland

Jerzy Skuratowicz

The term "transition" in the context of post-communist societies has become ambiguous from journalistic use and abuse. It is therefore necessary to state that I understand "transition" as a process of significant transformations in the operating principles and structures of the centralized model of physical allocation of resources, eliminating obstacles to efficiency and growth. In this sense, several attempts at transforming the economic system in Poland since 1956 have, by and large, proved unsuccessful because they were limited to modifications within the old framework.[1] Dramatic but swift change of the power elite in 1989 has removed political and ideological obstacles to the introduction of radical reforms aimed at the transformation of the existing economic system into that directed by the market through monetary instruments.

The market economies, however, despite their similar general features, have many faces and are not exactly the same in various countries. They are not solely defined by the "iron rules" of supply and demand but are also supported by complex systems of institutions shaping them. In the industrialized societies these institutions, consisting of private ownership, highly developed markets for production factors, and the organizational framework of the market economy, were gradually formed through centuries. The problems and difficulties during the transition process in Poland and other East European countries arise from the fact that market institutions must be created practically from scratch. Moreover, there is no country or group of countries in the contemporary world that can serve as a positive example of such transition.

Poland, along with Hungary, is the most advanced among the East European countries in institutional reforms paving the way to a market economy. Since the beginning of the 1980s, measures have been taken in Poland to liberalize gradually the prices of most commodities and services, controls over the activities of the private sector have been relaxed, and monetary reforms, instead of administrative guidance of the economy, have been gradually instituted.[2] However, drastic cuts in imports caused by balance-of-payments problems and the resulting shortages of industrial inputs slowed down the reforms. By the end of the decade, growing budget and balance-of-payments deficits led to accelerated inflation, which turned into hyperinflation.

The beginning of 1990 marked the introduction of a decisive stabilization policy, coupled with radical measures to transform the economic system. The effects so far have been mixed, and their assessment is far from unambiguous. On the one hand, restrictive monetary policy, the liberalization of most prices, the devaluation of national currency, and the introduction of a unified exchange rate have significantly reduced the rate of inflation, eliminated the huge budget deficit, stabilized the market for consumer goods, and generated a surplus in the foreign trade balance. A wide spectrum of new laws and regulations were passed in the parliament, opening the way to privatization and the expansion of individual entrepreneurship, development of capital and labor markets, and favorable conditions for foreign investors. On the other hand, an unprecedented drop in production of almost 30 percent, rising unemployment, a sharp decrease in real wages and consumption, modest results in the privatization process, and the reluctance of foreign capital to invest in Poland tarnish the positive aspects of the reforms.

The centralized model of physical allocation of resources has shown in the past a remarkable resistance to change. Due to this structural inertia, it seems pertinent to inquire into some of the problems and difficulties during the transition in Poland with regard to the responsiveness of the real economic system to monetary correction.

THE CONSEQUENCES OF RESTRICTIVE MONETARY POLICY DURING TRANSITION

It is correctly assumed that the transition to a market economy is hampered by macroeconomic instability and, in particular, by strong inflationary pressures distorting the correct relative prices. The stabilization program launched at the beginning of 1990 included severe budgetary and monetary restrictions in order to restrain aggregate demand and curb inflation. The negative impact of inflation on growth and efficiency was never underestimated in Poland, and during the 1980s, several programs were elaborated to strengthen the national currency and control inflation. They were largely unsuccessful, as they were limited in principle to the policy of wage and price controls without eliminating the structural sources of wasteful use of resources on the micro- and macroeconomic levels.

In the traditional central planning system, monetary policy was subordinated to the production targets, fixed, in general, on the principle of maximal utilization of production capacities.[3] Wage increases, bonuses, and other incentives for workers and management were directly linked to the execution of production targets without regard to efficiency. Within the system of price controls, high marginal costs of production and the general use of the cost-pricing method led to rising deficits of enterprises, which were financed by easy access to credit at negative interest rates guaranteed by the state budget.

Agriculture was also an important contributor to the budget deficit in Poland. This sector still employs 30 percent of the total work force and produces only 12 percent of GDP, indicating its low overall labor productivity. Consisting mainly of small family farms, agriculture needed relatively high capital inputs to intensify production, thus leading to the increase in the prices of food sold on the urban market. To contain the price rises on the one side, and to maintain the principle of income parity between rural and urban populations on the other, a complicated system of subsidies to the prices of food and to agricultural inputs was developed. This increased agriculture's share in budget expenditures.

All in all, subsidies constituted, in 1989, almost 40 percent of budget expenditures, of which more than half were for consumer prices and a quarter were to state enterprises. For a long time, internal imbalances generated pressure on wage increases, and a covert inflation manifested itself through shortages in the market of consumption goods and the discontinued supply of investment goods for the industrial sector. The liberalization of prices in the middle of 1989 turned covert into overt inflation.

A stabilization policy that restricts aggregate monetary demand through the control of domestic credit expansion should, according to theoretical assumptions, exert a double squeeze on the sources of the inflationary process. On the macroeconomic level, the elimination of the budget deficit by the reduction of subsidies should curtail monetary sources of inflation. On the microeconomic level, the enterprises would be forced to improve efficiency by adjusting their production to the levels determined by marginal costs and revenues. Units unable to adjust would be expected to close their doors and announce bankruptcy. Similar effects, although with a certain time lag, could be expected in agriculture, where the adjustment process should lead to a more efficient use of resources.

However, because of a highly monopolized industry in the state-owned sector, coupled with a low mobility of capital and labor, the response of the Polish economic system to monetary correction did not necessarily conform to theoretical assumptions. The more the government followed a restrictive monetary policy, the more the velocity of money increased. Enterprises reluctant to take credits at high interest rates, refusing to be squeezed out of existence, borrowed from each other to overcome their difficulties or perhaps to survive. Thus, the policy of positive and high interest rates lost much of its intended design. Moreover, recession did not initiate positive adjustment effects in the industrial structure. None of the inefficient steel mills, collieries, or shipyards went bankrupt. On the contrary, the steepest decline in production could be noted in consumption-goods industries such as textiles and garments, as well as in food-processing industries, which were important to the improvement of macroeconomic efficiency of the Polish economy. Industrial branches characterized by high capital-output ratios concentrated mainly in the extractive and intermediate goods industries fared relatively better.

Among the many explanations for this type of industrial sector adjustment to recession, the following seem of particular importance.

1. The high degree of monopolization of the industrial sector allowed many enterprises to reduce production and increase their prices.
2. Strong interbranch output and input links between extractive, intermediate, and final capital-goods industries created a protective shield against a sharp drop of demand for their products from other sectors of the economic system.
3. The structure of production costs gives bigger opportunities for survival during recession to enterprises with relatively higher shares of fixed costs and lesser opportunities to those with relatively higher variable costs.

At the same time, declining production forced enterprises to rationalize employment. New laws were introduced to eliminate formal rigidities in labor mobility. Many units started to reduce employment, bringing unemployment from almost zero to 1.2 million persons, or 10 percent of the total active work force in the state industrial sector by the end of 1990. However, the fall in production was faster than the fall in employment, worsening most of the economic indicators (for example, average fixed costs increased and labor productivity fell), and the inefficient industrial structure was not encroached upon. This type of response of the industrial sector seems to indicate that the success in curbing inflation through monetary restrictions may be of a short-lived nature.

Another important source of inflationary pressure in Poland comes from agriculture. Although 76 percent of land is private, the average farm size is very small. Almost 60 percent of all family farms are less than twelve acres, and half of those are less than five acres. Archaic farm size, low productivity of labor, and relatively high costs of agricultural production contribute to the overall low efficiency of this sector. Thus, the reforms leading to a market economy cannot exclude agriculture.

The first step for this sector in the introduction of a market economy was the liberalization of agricultural prices. The immediate effect was a sharp rise in food prices, which strongly affected real wages because food constitutes between 50 and 60 percent of urban family budget expenditures. This, in turn, led to a decline in demand for agricultural products, thus reducing the incomes of the farmers. As the main factors of production in agriculture—land, capital, and labor—are fixed, in the short run, a different reaction to the liberalization of prices could hardly have been expected. In the long run, as the literature shows, the deterioration of relative prices should lead to the concentration of farm land, raised productivity, and decreased costs.[4] At the same time, part of the labor force should move to other activities as labor mobility increases. Because of the existing features of the Polish agricultural sector, this process is unlikely to follow the general rules.

Above all, family farms, constituting the bulk of agricultural holdings, are characterized by a relatively high degree of self-sufficiency and are motivated by income rather than by profit maximization. Furthermore, the low level of indebtedness of the farmers does not expose them excessively to the fluctuations of interest rates, as is the case in the industrialized countries. The deterioration of relative prices and the fall in their revenue may only reduce the marketable share of their production.

A potential source of surplus land and labor resides in the group of the smallest farms (below five acres), which represents one-third of the total number of farms. Their low level of output and income is supplemented by seasonal employment outside agriculture or by social funds from the state budget. Cuts in budget spending and rising unemployment should expose them to the "iron rules" of the market, forcing them to sell their land. But in the existing economic environment, recession and low mobility caused by the shortage of housing attaches them even stronger to their farms.

The third group of big, and usually highly specialized, farms reacts to price movements in the same way as in the industrialized countries, but under different economic conditions. The worsening relative prices tend to depress their profits, but the fall in marketable surplus of the smaller family farms and relatively low price elasticity of demand for food products permit them to behave more like monopolists: They are able to offset the declining volume of sales by increasing prices.

Although the behavior of individual farms could have been further differentiated, suffice it to say that the agriculture sector as a whole responded to the liberalization of prices by reduced investment and a fall of output and income. At the same time, sharp rises in food prices significantly lowered the urban population's consumption.

Monetary policies do have a strong impact on agricultural production, investment, and income distribution, but they seem quite inefficient in transforming the agrarian structure. In the case of Polish agriculture, they contribute to the petrification of low-productivity farms rather than to strengthening the market-oriented and highly commercial ones.

ELEMENTS OF THE TRANSFORMING ECONOMY

The process of transition is not limited, of course, to the stabilization of the economy and to the dismantling of the centrally planned system but also, and perhaps above all, to the creation of general structures of a market economy. The scope of reforms is immense: It is necessary to demonopolize the economy, close inefficient plants, create a new financial and banking system, stimulate the development of the private sector, introduce modern management techniques, and create the necessary infrastructure of services, transport, and communication. But the effects will be negligible if the mobility of capital and labor is not enhanced.

The development of a market economy is certainly difficult where almost 80 percent of the value of production and services outside agriculture is state-owned. It is therefore claimed that the most important task in the transition to a market economy is to transfer state property into private hands, and this is where the process of reforms should start. The postulate of rapid and total privatization in Poland is, however, unrealistic. The problem hampering this process is that the society does not have enough money to buy state property. With an average yearly income equivalent to U.S. $1,800, most of the individual savings represent more of a deferred demand than investment capital. Moreover, the value of total savings held by the population in the banks is estimated to represent no more than 15 to 20 percent of the value of total fixed assets of the state industrial sector.

In Britain, where the level of income is, on the average, seven times higher than in Poland, where capital markets are well developed, and where the share of the public sector is much smaller, it is estimated that the process of total privatization would have to take from thirty to forty years. In Poland, in order to obtain the same transfer of state property into private hands, the process would last for a century.

What are the practical possibilities for the extension of the private sector? In the short run, the most promising procedure would be to encourage foreign capital investment and the "small privatization" in trade, leisure, other services, and small-scale industry. This would contribute to the reduction of excessive liquidity on the market, create new investment incentives, and encourage more efficient use of resources in these activities. Although the privatization of big state enterprises is difficult in the short run, it is possible to transform their assets into equity capital and submit them to public bidding. This, however, requires the creation of a stock exchange, which does not exist. Nevertheless, a small number of state enterprises have been transformed into stock companies and the shares have been sold on the open market. The results of this experience indicate a very strong dispersion of shares among a large number of small buyers, with the state treasury as the main stock holder. In the immediate future, the transformation of state enterprises into stock companies does not solve the problem of state property and control. It does, however, create conditions in the long run for mixed forms of ownership, including foreign investors.

A necessary condition of the transition process is the development of the labor market and the increased mobility of the work force. In the centrally planned system, labor mobility was largely restricted by a number of regulations limiting employment in the private sector and fixing upper limits on the size of farms in agriculture, by a relatively egalitarian income distribution, as well as by shortages in housing facilities. Based on the principle of full employment, economic and social policies discouraged the free movement of labor and created a rigid system of job security, often disregarding efficiency.

It is possible to implement several measures to increase mobility, such as a reduction of constraints in the housing sector and the development of unemployment offices. The most pressing problem, however, facing the Polish economy today and for the foreseeable future is the increase in the demand for labor rather than the increase in its supply.

The state industrial sector is unlikely to contribute in the near future to the growth of employment demand. The restructuring of the industrial sector should aim at the closing of a number of inefficient enterprises, mostly in the extractive and heavy industries, which employ almost three-quarters of the total work force of the state sector. The choices are certainly not easy to make. The fact that a number of plants—for instance, in the coal industry— produce at costs three to five times higher than in other plants exposes them to lockouts. Similar problems exist in many other branches, but at the same time, new investment is needed in textile, clothing, and food processing industries. These branches, using relatively unsophisticated and imported technologies, can contribute to the development of the private sector, the expansion of exports, and, because of low capital/employment ratios, the creation of new and relatively cheap job opportunities. The program of restructuring the industrial sector should be associated with the development of a modern financial system determining the same "rules of the game" for private and public sectors alike.

Nonetheless, in the immediate future, the process of rationalization of employment and restructuring suggests that the state industrial sector will be the most important source of labor supply to the rest of the economy. In 1990, the rate of growth of unemployment in this sector averaged 1.3 percent per month, or 17 percent per year, caused only by the rationalization of employment and recession. The expected closure of a number of inefficient enterprises will certainly increase the number of unemployed.

Agriculture will have its own employment problems related to the process of its modernization. As stated earlier, the possibilities of modernization of this sector leading to higher productivity are connected with the increase in the average size of farms and therefore an important reduction of employment in agricultural activities. At a reasonable, but high, rate of migration from agriculture of 4 percent a year, it would take ten years to bring down the share of this sector in total employment from the present 30 to 20 percent, a number that is still more than double West European standards. In the immediate future, however, the rest of the national economy is not prepared for this process. The restructuring of the industrial sector will inevitably create serious unemployment problems with financial strains on the state budget for some time to come. Some of the former farmers may find employment in services in the countryside, but others will probably join the urban labor market. An additional flow of migrants from agriculture may only aggravate the situation in the labor market and put at risk the process of reforming the economic system as a whole. It therefore seems appropriate to seek a set of monetary and fiscal policies that could create the economic conditions necessary to slow down rather than increase the mobility of labor in agriculture until industry and services solve their own problems of employment and are ready to provide work for the migrants.

The only sector that could eventually be relied on to absorb the surplus labor from all sources is the private manufacturing and service sector. The contribution of the private sector to employment is very limited in the first stages of the transition process, not only because of its small share in overall employment and output, but also because of the size of capital involved and its dispersion among a large number of owners. It contributes 10 percent to total output outside agriculture, employs 14 percent of the labor force, and owns 2.2 percent of the total value of fixed assets. Moreover, over 50 percent of those working in the private sector are self-employed. A simple calculation indicates that the increase in employment rate necessary for the absorption of entrants to the labor market coming from the restructured state sector and from the population growth of 0.8 percent a year would require the growth of employment opportunities in the private sector at an annual rate of over 100 percent. Even in the case of the very simple, labor-intensive technologies in use in the private sector, such a growth rate of employment is quite unrealistic.

The private sector is too small and economically too weak to undertake and lead the enormous task of breaking monopolies, transforming in a civilized way the ownership structures, modernizing the economy, developing the capital and labor markets, and rationalizing the financial and banking system.

TOWARD A MORE RATIONAL MACROECONOMIC POLICY

For a long time to come, the system of state enterprises will remain the core of the economy. The transformation of this system is of paramount importance for the success or failure of reforms in industry, agriculture, and services.[5] The reform of the state sector can play a central role in stimulating production, employment, and demand in other sectors, including the private one. In the long run, it can contribute to a more efficient use of resources.

From this point of view, it seems important to note that the transition process should not concentrate only on the objective of replacing the old command system by the market system but also must include the objective of modernization of the economic structure. The simultaneous restructuring of the entire economy in a relatively short time may be very costly and can undermine social support for the whole process.

The above-mentioned aspects of the transition process involve changes in the attitude of policy-making bodies toward wages and growth. The economic policy should reverse the established tendency of financing growth through the contraction of real wages and consumption. This growth model, typical of many less developed countries, is one of the main impediments to the creation of a demand-driven market economy. In the industrialized countries, wages and salaries constitute the most important part of the national income and demand. In Poland, only about 40 percent of the national income and 60 percent of total consumption depend directly on income related to work. The rest is distributed through different channels from the state budget or enterprise social funds in the form of collective consumption, that is, through funds controlled by the state and unrelated directly to work. Taxes on household income and from the private sector represent less than 10 percent of budget revenue. The relatively small contribution of wages to national income and to budget revenue creates a situation in which the basic component of national demand is composed of income of the state industrial sector. Considering that wages represent between 8 and 16 percent of total production costs in the industrial state sector, the often-raised argument of the wage-push inflation may be of little practical value. Thus, on the one hand, the struggle against inflation by the contraction of wages may actually lead to the adjustment of monetary demand to the distorted production structures. On the other hand, the efforts to increase financial efficiency of enterprises through the fall in personal incomes may create serious problems affecting the long-term development process. The deterioration of relative prices of labor and capital may not stimulate the growth of productivity. If technology becomes more expensive than labor, the enterprises—whether state or privately owned—will be able to improve their financial standing by using low-paid workers instead of modern technology.

According to the theoretical model, such a situation cannot last for long. Whether on a national or international scale, market adjustment mechanisms should start to work. The hopes for higher profits resulting from low wages and higher prices, both being the result of low productivity in underdeveloped regions or countries, should attract capital, raise productivity, and bring development. It is certainly difficult to contradict this tendency in different periods of history. But it is also difficult to contradict the existence of an opposite tendency. The theoretical model does not consider a situation in which the remuneration of labor would be lower than its productivity. Because of the structural inertia of the Polish economy, the great challenge during the transition process is to avoid the situation that could be best described as "impoverishing growth."

The fundamental problems confronting the policy-making bodies are to formulate and execute coherent programs that accelerate the reforms oriented to the creation of a market economy and avoid at the same time two obvious traps. The first is the risk of slowing down the reforms due to the resistance of the existing structures to changes. The second is the risk associated with the unexpected and inappropriate response of the structures to monetary corrections, which can lead to political and economic instability.

As macroeconomic stabilization must be associated with the general transformation of the system, all aspects of the reform program can be considered as being of utmost urgency. In the real economic world, however, policy choices are usually limited by scarce resources. On the one hand, in order to accelerate the reforms, Poland will surely need relief in its debt and the assistance of the international community. On the other hand, it is necessary to determine the timing, costs, and sequence of reforms in different fields of economic activity in order to achieve a durable growth and long-term development in the context of the market system. The determination of priorities evidently goes against the basic principles of a market-regulated economic system. But are market rules of the game efficient in an economic system that lacks fundamental market institutions? The view expressed here is that there is little chance for the transition from a centrally planned economy to a market-oriented economy in an evolutionary way without a conscious and active role of the state.

CONCLUSION

Experience shows that the course of economic reforms is seldom smooth. The fact that in Poland market institutions are virtually non-existent adds to the scope and intensity of problems during the transition process. Thus, the necessity of creating appropriate institutions of a market economy and the relatively low response of existing structures to monetary correction demand a conscious and active government involvement in determining the timing, costs, and sequence of reforms. Most economic decisions involve a good deal of risk the further they go beyond the problems generally associated with macroeconomic stabilization and adjustment policies, as they imply profound transformation in the political and social life of the country. The key question is: How will the economic system react when even the most reasonable decisions are overtaken by unexpected events? Anne Krueger noted that the success or failure of reforms depends largely on the speed with which policy makers recognize their mistakes and deal with them.[6] This remark seems to be of particular relevance to the policy choices during the transition process in Poland.

J. Skuratowicz

NOTES

1. For an interesting historical presentation of attempts to reform the Polish economy, see Brus (1988).

2. For an extensive analysis of the Polish economy in the first half of the 1980s, see World Bank (1987).

3. For an extensive analysis of the centrally planned system, see Kornai (1980).

4. For an assessment of the short- and long-run response of agriculture to prices, see Binswanger (1989).

5. For a similar approach to the role of the state sector during the transition, see Wapenhans (1990).

6. For an assessment of policy choices in development, see Krueger (1987).

Chapter 6

Macroeconomic Policy and Institutions in the Czechoslovak Transition: The Starting Point and First Steps

Ales Bulir

The purpose of this chapter is to examine the institutional background of recent developments in Czechoslovakia and to suggest the design of future changes. The attempt of Czechoslovak reformers is to realize a rapid transition to a market economy. On the way to the market, though, several obstacles must be overcome.

One is usually interested in what is to be transformed, the timing of the process, and so forth. However, serious misunderstandings can evolve if the background of the previous institutional arrangements and macroeconomic performance is not understood. Such a description will be contained in the first part of this chapter, with special attention to the macroeconomic dimensions of a closed economy. The second part will address institutional changes and institutional prerequisites of a new macroeconomic policy. The third part is concerned with specific problems concerning monetary and fiscal policy in the transition.

BASIC CHARACTERISTICS OF A CENTRALLY PLANNED ECONOMY

It is not surprising that the monetary and fiscal systems of communist countries differ fundamentally from the corresponding arrangements in the West. What is usually referred to as the standard command system, including the basic communist concepts regarding the role of banks in the economy, first took shape in the Soviet Union during the early 1930s and then was introduced into the other eastern bloc countries when they came under communist control after World War II. The policy outlines were not altered significantly among the individual countries. Nevertheless, the fact that certain procedures or institutional arrangements were used, say, in Czechoslovakia or in the Soviet Union, does not mean that they were employed elsewhere. Although the Soviet Union was the prototype for the other eastern bloc countries, some elements of the Western economic culture have survived to a surprising degree in a number of these countries. Still, it is possible and beneficial to summarize basic principles concerning these topics that have a certain general validity.

Regardless of the country and possible reform attempts, the basic features of centrally planned economies remained intact for the last 40 years. Production targets, formulated mainly in physical terms, were embodied in the form of output plans. Designated governmental agencies specified for each enterprise, or group of enterprises, sources and quantities of basic inputs. Key prices were fixed by authorities, and wage rates and total payroll costs were also strictly controlled. Allocation of resources was determined by the central plan and not through the price system.[1] Private ownership of the means of production was destroyed, and financial markets and their instruments were abolished. Administrative measures, and not market adjustments, were used to correct disequilibria. Inconvertibility of the domestic currency derived necessarily from a system of centralized decision making since the planning model required that authorities retain a monopoly over foreign trade and foreign exchange. The inevitable result of inconvertibility is to isolate an economy from the rest of the world and to prevent the price system from transmitting relevant information.

Despite proclamations of Soviet economists in the early 1920s, the money and banking systems did not disappear. Also, taxes and the public economy were not replaced by direct material allocation. Fiscal and monetary authorities compiled their own one-year and five-year plans, but these were only complements to material plans. These institutions and their policies are hard to evaluate in Western dimensions. Since almost all basic planning was in real magnitudes, so-called material balances, the role of money was to provide a common denominator for aggregation.[2] Banks acted to ensure the smoothness of the planned path of economic expansion, regardless of profits or liquidity. The scope for a relatively independent monetary policy opened in Czechoslovakia after 1980, and even then, monetary authorities were under strong pressure from state authorities.

The position of fiscal authorities was even weaker because their aim was to provide a rigid set of public goods and administrative redistributions. Public goods proceeded from "implanted" values (free health and educational services, full employment, centralized social insurance, etc.)

rather than as the result of public choice. With respect to the decreased efficiency of socialist economies, both in absolute and comparative terms, the quality of these services has fallen.

FINANCIAL INSTITUTIONS

One can identify three central authorities in the socialist economies: the planning authority, the monetary authority, and the fiscal authority. The most influential of these is the planning authority, which is beyond the scope of this chapter. Let us start with the more important of the two remaining institutions: fiscal authority and the government budget.

Government Budget

From the beginning of socialist construction in the 1950s, almost all financial flows in the production sector, either related to the movement of final goods or to the flow of investment, were influenced by material output and input plans. Financial flows were not market determined; indeed, there were neither capital markets nor profit-maximizing commercial banks that could have allocated these scarce resources. Government institutions functioned without public control, and thus their instruments became "fuzzy" (Zieleniec 1990).

Instead, all major macroeconomic decisions—such as the division of current output between consumption and investment and allocative measures between industry and agriculture, or among industries, regions, and social groups—were embodied in the government budget. In the 1950s and 1960s, approximately 90 percent of the financial counterpart of the flow of real resources into investment was channelled through the budget. (Below we will show why this tight relationship disappeared in the 1970s and 1980s.) Also, a large proportion of consumption was channelled through the budget. The ratio of the government budget relative to net material product[3] grew steadily (a decrease of investment expenditures was offset by other expenses), and in Czechoslovakia in 1989, this proportion exceeded 70 percent, higher than in any Western country.

On the revenue side, the main resources were profit taxes and redistribution of depreciation, and only 10 to 12 percent of revenue was taxes paid by the population—numbers quite unusual by Western standards. These were popular measures, and wages could remain low. Moreover, the role of indirect taxes was steadily decreasing over time. The Ministry of Finance had no need to be afraid about funding sources, as the constitution enabled it to levy a new tax or increase the rate of an existing tax on state enterprises in order to balance its current budget. This was often done in the 1980s.

The position of the government budget resulted from two features. First, the channelling through the budget of the bulk of all investment in the 1950s enabled the reconstruction of heavy industry, and later, the concentration of resources into preferred industries. Second, the financing of a very large part of expenditures in so-called collective consumption, which included not only free education, health or other social services, but also enormous subsidies for food[4], housing, transportation, and so on, constituted a major use of funds.

This colossal burden, which led to hidden budget deficits in the 1980s, was above all an attempt to convince the population about the possibility of an improved standard of living and a successful way to communism. For political reasons, the built-in growth rate of expenditures into collective consumption offset the growth rate of expenditures into investment, environmental activities, and, in fact, led to a large capital deficit in the form of obsolete industry and infrastructure, pollution, and so on. Some economists therefore like to speak about the debt against capital, the so-called borrowing from the future. This debt is indeed impossible to express in exact monetary terms.

The accelerating rate of growth of expenditures for collective consumption (due to, for example, more expensive basic medical equipment, a higher share of retired population, or simply bureaucratic expenses) caused pressures on the budget balance in the 1970s and 1980s. But the Ministry of Finance never ran an open deficit and even when there where signs of it, the deficit was monetized: The expenditures were moved into the monobank's operations and these expenditures were covered by monobank's loans (Bulir 1990). Because political forces in the Communist Party preferred, for political reasons, expenditures for social purposes, this led finally to a decrease of financing for investment.

One can also see fundamental microeconomic issues connected with the public finance process. These issues, however, go far beyond the scope of this chapter. Some useful points can be found in Wiles (1979).

However, this accounting change did not mean a decentralization or even "marketization" of the investment process, as financial sources were simply channelled through the monobank rather than through the budget.

The Monobank

The particular form of banking organization developed originally in the Soviet Union combined in the state bank some attributes of a central bank with those functions of commercial banking that were relevant in a communist country. The main reasons for merging deposit and central banks into a monobank can be found in Wiles (1979: 312). The term "monobank" well describes this type of banking structure, even though the monobank was supplemented by a small number of specialized banks, including an "investment" bank, a savings bank, and a foreign trade bank. The important feature of the system was that all these banks were monopolies in their specific areas.

In specific terms, the monobank was the bank of issue. It managed foreign exchange reserves in close cooperation with and, in some cases, under the direction of the Ministry of Finance and the Ministry of Foreign Trade. The monobank was the sole source of short-term (and, in the 1970s and 1980s, also of long-term) credit, as the extension of direct interenterprise credit was forbidden.

Since control of credit was exercised directly, setting the credit limit for the economy and limits for individual branches, the monobank was not concerned with controlling the reserves of commercial banks or with open-market operations as central banks in Western countries are.

The monobank also served as the settlement and clearing center of the country (e.g., it had to solve liquidity problems of firms) and performed all the usual fiscal agency functions carried out by central banks in the West. Credit limits in the branches of the state bank were directly derived from plans of individual enterprises in material units, and firms were given credit or other resources for financing particular activities. Because payment flows and credit allocation were planned and tied to plan fulfillment, all such monobank operations involved an audit function to check conformity of payments to underlying authorization, called "control by the *koruna.*"[5]

In addition, in the 1980s, the monobank in Czechoslovakia tried to provide a non-inflationary monetary policy.[6] This included credit targeting and a certain decentralization of direct credit allocation. Nevertheless, it is extreme to say that the credit rationing system was abandoned (Goodhart 1989: Chap. 7). However, during those attempts, the main problems connected with the monobank and with the impossibility of a tight monetary policy arose and became apparent: the "fuzzy" objective function of the monobank and the demonetization of the economy.

First, part of the problem stemmed from rules under which the monobank was established. Once the plan was accepted, the monobank's objectives were directed toward keeping the monetary variables in line with the projections that related changes in credit to the material targets. Money was put into circulation only to support the movement of goods.

The primary goal of the monobank was to financially secure the production process. Thus, the monobank was an adjuster, not a steerer. And it is well known that objectives promoting accommodative policy and anti-inflationary policy are contradictory.

Second, the separation of households from producers (no shares and no private capital ownership) led to different developments in the household and firm sectors. These included different price indices, different structures of commodities supplied to firm and household markets, different currency-demand deposit ratios, and even dissimilar responses to monetary impulses.[7] These features are sometimes described as a "hard" budget constraint within the household sector and a "soft" budget constraint within the producer sector. A soft budget constraint implies that liquidity is not the central aim of a socialist firm. Developments in the 1980s during tight monetary policy periods seem to confirm this statement: Many large firms have survived even in a permanent state of "payment incapability."

The consequences of such developments, which lasted over decades, are sometimes surprising: elimination of interest rates (the real interest rate was, in many cases, zero), relations between particular interest rates that appeared arbitrary, and non-homogeneous money supply. It was meaningless to sum up the currency in the hands of the public and the current accounts used by enterprises as they bore no significant connection to the development of aggregate indicators of economic performance. The same can be said about the exchange rate and the behavior of firms. Government budgets, directly via export subsidies, and the state bank, indirectly via a fixed exchange rate system, determined foreign trade.

MACROECONOMIC OR MICROECONOMIC POLICY?

Following the description in the previous section of the basic principles of the fiscal and monetary systems, there arise crucial questions: Did there exist any macroeconomic policy in the classical sense in Czechoslovakia and in other communist countries? Were decisions about government outlays based on either explicit or implicit estimates of the expenditure multiplier? Did the state bank have any idea about demand for money functions and were they used for managing price stability? Did the exchange rate contribute to competitiveness of the economy and to the equilibrium of the balance of payment? The general, slightly oversimplified, answer is no.

One may wonder what the reasons were in most Comecon countries, especially in Czechoslovakia, for the relatively good macroeconomic performance: zero unemployment, a rate of growth of official price indices close to zero, a rate of growth of net material product above relevant figures of OECD countries in the 1950s and 1960s and comparable to them in the 1970s.[8] Only in the 1980s was there a significant slowdown in the growth rate and rise in price levels.

The key to understanding economic policy and the performance of a communist country lies in the abandonment of the macroeconomic dimension of government interference. State activities, either from the monetary or from the fiscal side, were not neutral. Rather, they were focused on particular firms or regions, particular products, or particular social issues. Thus, the federal government never discussed any macroeconomic issue. The evidence shows that the economy was managed by microeconomic interference rather than by macroeconomic. These microeconomic interferences contained price management, the directive credit rationing system, a wide system of subsidies and centralized redistribution, or simply commands.

One may ask what enabled central authorities to provide such a policy. This can be explained using the concept of property rights. Nobody owned anything, but many could make decisions. The original normative idea of creating a socialist economy was based on the assumption that there would be no agents that maximized their own profits. Instead of creating fixed rules of behavior and leaving the values of variable parameters—above all, prices and optimal plans—to the market, the socialist state tried to directly influence parameters, prices, and outcomes, and almost completely resigned from the role of affecting the rules.

The lack of a macroeconomic dimension in government policy enabled the communist countries in the short run, above all in the 1950s, to reach some surprising results, such as in the areas of industrialization or electrification. Nevertheless, in the long run, the system was extremely ineffective. Good long-term economic performance in Comecon countries is partly myth and data falsification, partly the result of hidden and repressed inflation, and partly the creation of an inner debt against capital, nature, infrastructure, and so on.

Some effects of the declining growth capacity of economy were hidden, but they have emerged clearly in the 1980s. The decentralization of decision making during perestroika negatively affected the centralized allocation, which was ineffective but at least consistent. Decentralization and macroeconomic policy could not create positive results without solving the problem of "fuzzy" property rights. Problems connected with the insufficient legal framework, the creation of which might be even more important than policy, have been discussed in Brenner (1990).

CENTRALLY PLANNED ECONOMIES AND INFLATION

Unfortunately, there is a common belief among Western economists that centrally planned economies have had lower inflation rates, which they believed implied that a government with particularly strong power would not choose inflation as a means of raising additional resources (see, for example, Goodhart 1989: 44). In the case of Czechoslovakia, they even talk about "monetary virginity."

These authors do not consider hidden and repressed inflation, as in Klaus (1989). The core of the problem is that we must look at the cost of inflation and not at the inflation rate itself. Inflation is likely to be far more costly than simple considerations of the welfare loss on money balances suggest, as in Garfinkel (1989). Communist economies were subject to situations where individual prices and the price level did not react to excess demand because of fixed prices. Prices, in fact, did not fulfill the allocative function. Costs of hidden and repressed inflation are not very often mentioned in the literature, and it would be useful to repeat them here.

The inflation processes in the East and West had one main difference. In the West, particular markets (for food, cars, electronics, housing, etc.) were in equilibria; in the East, they were not. Microeconomic disequilibria suspended competition; in these markets, even "lemons" were tradeable. Typical reactions of suppliers have been to lower the quality, narrow the production assortment, offer bribes, and ration. This was relatively easy because there was no free entry, and most firms were monopolists. However, both consumers and producers were facing high search costs and the term "hoarding" accurately describes their behavior.[9]

But what many economists evaluate as the main dangers are indirect (behavioral) effects of hidden and repressed inflation: The behavior of agents differs from their behavior in the partial market equilibrium. Missing is the connection between the income and the purchasing power, as goods are simply not available in the appropriate quantities and/or assortments. Disequilibrium and hidden and repressed inflation increase uncertainty for a producer, who does not know the goods' prices or whether the inputs will be available.

In Czechoslovakia, as in other Comecon countries, this condition reduced all long-term activities: Firms followed short-term benefits, households preferred consumption to savings.[10] What is substantial is the fact that the behavioral defects cannot be removed very quickly.

It is not necessary to emphasize that such a broadly defined inflationary development is not solvable with macroeconomic tools, which can only slow down the conversion from hidden and repressed inflation to an open inflation during the adjustment process. Partial disequilibria cannot be removed by cutting aggregate demand without associated supply-side improvements. (Straightforward price adjustments could be in some cases socially unacceptable.) During the transition period, the increase of the price level could be driven partially (in the case of accommodative monetary policy) and almost entirely (in the case of non-accommodative policy) by the adjustment of relative prices rather than aggregate price changes.[11]

The purpose of the previous sections has been to show the current state of affairs in Czechoslovakia and their institutional background. Comments on inflation should emphasize that Czechoslovakia might face, at the beginning of its transformation, more problems than are visible from crude macroeconomic figures.[12]

CHANGES IN FINANCIAL INSTITUTIONS

The basic assumption underlying the process of sharp transformation is that in the background are the necessary institutions. The core of the transformation is unmistakably the privatization of the economy. Nevertheless, there is one crucial institutional task that has a strong connection to monetary economics: the creation of a sound banking and financial system. Accordingly, this feature could cause even more problems than privatization. A sound financial system is the precondition for future growth and its absence will cause stagnation. A period of three years to create a normal, functioning system of commercial banking does not seem long enough.

Until the end of 1989, the Czechoslovak banking sector was functioning under the monopoly of the state bank. Since 1950, this bank (a monobank) had fulfilled the role of a central bank as well as the role of commercial banks. There were some specialized banks, such as the Czechoslovak Trade Bank, a stock company (shareholders were domestic foreign trade companies and the state bank), and two very small, state-owned banks— the entrepreneurial bank, which provided foreign exchange payments for domestic households, and the investment bank, which managed securities owned by Czechoslovak households (mostly shares and bonds bought before World War II).[13] The last two banks played only a fringe role in economic life. The great monopolistic thrift institutions, Czech and Slovak saving banks, received deposits at fixed interest rates and lent them to the monobank. This system constituted the entire banking structure until the end of 1989.

Readers may find useful a short review of the basic features of that system:

1. Complete monopolization of the system, aimed at certain customers and certain sorts of banking services. (This is not the same as specialization based on economies of scale.) The banking sector was serving as a centralized redistributor of financial claims and was not providing the role of financial intermediation.

2. Low endowment of equity capital as the state budget guaranteed all credits and deposits, and the state banks could not fail.

3. Huge amount of credits with default (credit) risk, many of them being without term to maturity.

4. Insufficient volume and quality of banking services and the low density of branches.

5. A low number of employees (approximately five or six times less than in West Germany).

The first step was the transformation of the monobank into a system of a central bank and commercial banks. The idea was to establish competition in the banking sector and create a space for macroeconomic policy for the state bank.

There is nothing special about the central bank. The state bank should simply provide a very prudential, non-accommodative monetary policy. The likely intermediate targets are a zero rate of growth of real money supply[14] intervention to stabilize the exchange rate.

The assets and liabilities of the monobank that are not necessary for the future central bank have been split between two newly established, state-owned commercial banks and an enlarged investment bank. These intermediaries were created as universal banks. During 1990, some independent banks were also established. The new, state-owned banks suffer from the heritage of the previous monobank, and the independent banks suffer from a weak network and a lack of skilled employees.

The main brake on the unexpectedly slow development within the banking sector is the inconsistent legal framework for establishing and running new banks, bureaucratic barriers to entry and, above all, technical difficulties and low capital endowment. Even the current state of infrastructure does not allow for the creation of a modern bank. One possible solution, which has been widely used, is the creation of joint ventures with Western banks, especially from Germany, Austria, and France. This should shorten the way, both in terms of technology and retraining.

Can an economy be privatized without knowing the market prices of shares? How will these shares be traded after the first allocation through vouchers? Should the vouchers be neutral to the government budget? What about the inflationary impacts of this process? How will the central bank maintain its targets without open market operations? Most of these questions will be answered by practical experience in the very near future; however, we see that problems the banking system is facing create one of the bottlenecks of the transition.

ECONOMIC POLICY IN THE TRANSITION: SOME ASPECTS

There are no doubts about the definite aims of current policy: to realize the transition from a centrally planned economy to a market economy. Czechoslovakia wants to achieve the transition from a state-dominated economy to an economy based on private initiative and private property. In a short period of time, Czechoslovakia would like to be a member of the European Community.

There are few doubts about the appropriate instruments for achieving this. The instruments will be touched on later, but let us briefly mention the conditions. The reform process must build and maintain new political and social consensus within the society and, at the same time, break down the old, unproductive, and collectivistic social contract. All measures should minimize the cost of restructuring the system in terms of growth, employment, and inflation. At the same time, the government must both maintain the credibility of the reform process and not cross the tolerance limit of the population.[15]

Another important fact to be mentioned is the external environment. Most projections of the speed of the transition suppose that the economic growth rate as from the middle of 1980s will continue. Furthermore, the disintegration of Comecon and the general decline of foreign trade among these countries will require an opposite increase in trade with developed countries. What is demanded is thus both free entry to foreign markets and foreign direct investment. There are strong incentives for Western politicians to ensure this, and it seems that many of them do appreciate this challenge. If reforms in the East should fail, it will affect the West as well because it would create a new center of instability.

Until now, we have not paid attention to the foreign exchange transactions and to the balance of payments. Czechoslovakia is sharply distinguished from the other Comecon countries by its low level of international debt; the U.S. $8 billion debt at the end of 1990 is easy to support at current export levels. The reform blueprint does not expect a rapid increase of that debt. Economic programs should be supported by foreign direct investment, and convertibility should be maintained using standby credit from the International Monetary Fund (IMF).[16] The example of Polish foreign debt and hyperinflation is probably a sufficient warning to its neighbors.

Both final and intermediate targets are known, and there are no substantial doubts about appropriate policies. Authorities, at the same time, know the necessary conditions. Is there any problem?

One may say that the main issue is proper sequencing. For example, is it useful to liberalize all prices at a time when the huge majority of firms are state owned and, above all, while most of them are monopolies? Is it necessary to liberalize foreign trade? And if so, how will that influence the balance of payments? Or, should privatization of the whole economy precede price liberalization?

There are, however, no definite answers and no advanced prepared patterns. Managing these issues will demand careful, up-to-date measures in both the macroeconomic and institutional frameworks. Let us focus on some of them.

The general task is to replace the above-described microeconomic policies with real macroeconomic policy, in other words, the transition from discretionary government interferences to rules. The main and immediate task is to reduce inflationary expectations[17] using prudent and restrictive macroeconomic policy. In presenting a surplus budget for 1990 and zero-growth monetary target, the government has indicated the importance it attaches to the control of inflation.[18]

These measures, however, would not be very successful in the long run if the current institutional framework is preserved. Enterprises would continue to operate in an environment where competition is lacking and would take advantage of their strong bargaining positions, and simply do "business as usual." More sophisticated macroeconomic policies demand institutional changes, including the changing role of the state. The standard reform program falls then into two parts: (1) a package of measures that should be undertaken promptly and simultaneously, since sustaining success in some areas will be heavily influenced by progress in others; and (2) a set of longer-term policy and institutional changes that are needed to complement the initial stage.

There is a common agreement that the first package, which should be introduced as soon as the necessary preparation can be made, should include:

1. Price liberalization, covering a wide range of domestic prices of all goods that are produced under reasonably competitive conditions. It is very likely that some basic (and politically sensitive) prices will be controlled or subsidized. Total coverage of goods initially affected by the price regulations, however, will amount only to 15 percent of total output.

2. Limited convertibility within the current account for domestic residents for the Czechoslovak *koruna*. This includes the liberalization of merchandise exports and imports, free repatriation of profits, and other current account operations, as well as the establishment of a unified exchange rate responsive to supply and demand.[19]

3. An adequately financed social safety program (a "social safety net") is required to meet the needs of individuals who become unemployed or otherwise suffer as a result of the adjustment process. Approximately 50 or 60 percent of the employee's wage ought to be guaranteed. This budgetary expense would have to be constrained by both the balanced budget and the need to encourage labor force mobility.

4. State-owned enterprises should be commercialized and an incentive system for managers should be introduced. The attitude of "business as usual" must not continue. Forcing firms into a certain level of financial discipline could help reduce inflationary pressures limiting both interenterprise loans and unofficial wage bargaining.

5. Foreign direct private investment should be encouraged, particularly in joint ventures, as Western firms are afraid to do business without using "insider" information.

The above items were the basic measures that could be promptly introduced. Legal preparation had been made mainly in 1990 and the package was started on January 1, 1991. These steps must be implemented even if there is a risk of insufficient legal framework and lack of institutions.

The second package should cover privatization, the changing role of the state, and restructuralization, or even the creation of institutions and governmental authorities that are necessary for a market economy. One can see that there is a reliable pattern for these changes—the developed economies and the IMF's advice. The remaining part of this package contains long-run policies that must support the supply side of the economy. These include energy and a foreign trade strategy, as well as development programs for agriculture.

A majority of economists believe that it is impossible to leave these roles entirely to the market because ours is not a competitive market, and the risk of market failure seems to be very high. On the one hand, the economy needs competition, which could be started by dividing state-owned monopolistic firms. On the other hand, some small firms would not be able to exploit economies of scale and distribution networks. These longer-term policies with microeconomic dimensions must be extremely flexible and allow for discretionary measures.

Let us again focus on monetary and fiscal policy.

Fiscal Policy

Balanced fiscal accounts or, at least, sustainable deficits are an important precondition for successful transition. Czechoslovakia should not start with contractionary stabilization policies. In 1990, it reached a small surplus of about 1 percent of net material product. However, the radical transformation, especially the separation of enterprises from the budget and the redistribution of functions between the state and the private sector, will result in huge shifts in budgetary accounts. A part of these shifts is due to the attempt to strengthen the confidence of the public by "making the budget clear."

On the revenue side, the government is going to lose direct access to profits of privatized firms, and the private firms' taxation is likely to be initially lower. However, one can expect wage increases in the private sector, both because of its desire to attract skilled labor, and the likely lack of hitherto freely provided or subsidized collective consumption: health and education services, prices of some necessities, and so on. Generally speaking, wages are expected to rise, and profits may be low in the initial years. For these reasons, the share of taxed enterprise profits and cooperative income taxes in total revenue is likely to decrease, while the share of payroll taxes can be expected to increase.

On the expenditure side, considerable funds must be spent on infrastructure, on modernizing the obsolete facilities in the public sector, and last, but definitely not least, on reducing environmental damage. There have been large cuts in direct subsidies, which amounted to 16 percent of the net material product (NMP) in 1988, but the social safety net costs are expected to rise as unemployment increases.

On the threshold of the transition process, it is difficult to predict the net fiscal outcome of all changes. Much will depend on the speed of reforms and public economy programs, as well as on the emergence of a strong private sector and foreign direct investment. The enormous risk that the budget will come increasingly under pressure, which will result in monetized deficits and, finally, inflation, can be avoided with a prudent expenditure policy and the introduction of new tax measures. These measures should emerge in the tax reform, which will come fully into operation in the mid-1990s.

Monetary and Credit Policy

The challenge of implementing sound monetary policy—regardless of the prewar tradition—is non-trivial for several reasons. First, the banking system, in the beginning of the 1990s, is not capable of moving from a system of direct credit allocation to one of indirect allocation based on interest rates, reserve requirements, and open market operations. Second, a delicate balance must be sought between supporting positive supply reactions, demanding loans—especially by private and privatized firms— and excessive credit and liquidity expansion. Third, monetary authority will have to distinguish between changes in the aggregate price index, as a result of relative price adjustments, and real inflationary pressures, either from the "demand-pull" or domestic "cost-push" sides or resulting from exchange rate devaluations (See Hafer 1989).

For the next few years, until a modern banking system emerges, monetary policy will be executed using both indirect measures and commands. First, the authorities intend to keep domestic credit expansion in real terms within the range of -2 percent to 1 percent and, at the same time, the state bank will maintain the discount rate so as to make it positive in real terms.

Second, the directive measures consist of maximum limits on refinancing (discount) credit for each bank, prudent ratios of reserves to total assets, and of outstanding medium- and long-term loans to corresponding deposits. All banks have to raise their required reserves with the state bank and inform it when loans to one client exceed a certain level, which will be subject to change, or when its total exposure to one client exceeds 50 percent of the capital and reserves of the bank. All commercial banks will be asked to increase their equity capital/total assets ratio by an agreed date. The extensive use of "gentlemen's agreements" between commercial banks and central authorities is also expected. In fact, the authorities have little choice but to continue, initially, to intervene directly in credit allocation in order to balance concerns over inflation and supply responses. Rationing in credit markets must be phased out as the commercial banking sector develops.

The advantage of relatively large voluntary household savings will be supported by increasing the interest rates and widening savings opportunities. In the past, Czechoslovakia has not suffered from the aggregate and/or lasting imbalances in consumer markets. Partial and temporary shortages (revealing repressed inflation) did arise, but there was always a possibility of substitution.

Nevertheless, we may be concerned about the reaction of the population. Once prices have been liberalized, extensive dissaving could disorganize all markets. A combination of positive interest rates, new incentives for saving, and a prudent wage policy should prevent an extensive demand push. Because the population expects substantial structural unemployment, one may anticipate a cautious approach to consumption.

A part of monetary policy will also be exchange rate management. The establishment of limited convertibility of the *koruna* (liberalization of buying and selling foreign exchange for current account transactions and a unified exchange rate) should provide the main information for export and import activities. The government intention is to intervene on the market to limit fluctuations outside of the specified range of a real exchange rate (especially in the case of rapid depreciation of koruna) to avoid sending confusing signals to producers as well as to reduce additional inflationary pressures. These measures require, of course, substantial reserves and stand-by credit, in the short run, and the rapid improvement of the foreign trade performance in the medium term, which would help to ensure an adequate supply of foreign exchange in the interbank market.

CONCLUSION

The purpose of this chapter was to show the current state of affairs in Czechoslovakia, the background of recent developments, and the macroeconomic design of future changes. Czechoslovakia wants to realize the transition from a centrally planned economy to a market economy and, in this respect, the reform intentions and instruments are quite clear and "standard." Leading reformers do not want to repeat the mistakes from previous reform attempts by introducing some hybrid system between central planning and a market economy.

This chapter showed both internal and external preconditions of the successful transition and some reform traps and weak spots at the macroeconomic and institutional levels that might be hidden from outsiders. Special attention was paid to monetary and fiscal policy and institutional changes. In the last section, the main measures that are expected to be implemented in those areas in the short and medium term were discussed.

NOTES

I thank Saul Estrin, Paul A. Greeman, Jiri Jones, Martin Mandel, Michal Mejstrik, and Zdenek Tuma for their comments on earlier drafts of the chapter. They provided me with many interesting details and ideas during the writing process. The responsibility for all mistakes and inaccuracies is, of course, exclusively mine.

1. The price system existing for the last forty years was based on average, instead of marginal costs. The most visible example of it was the exchange rate system; the exchange rate was set according to the average cost of producing U.S. $1 of output within the Czechoslovak exporting industries. A first-year student can define the resulting misallocation.

2. Monetary measures simply played the passive, accounting role, and the economy, at least in certain parts, functioned as a barter economy.

3. We will use net material product (NMP), the most widely used measure in Comecon countries, which is close to the national income. The use of NMP was mainly the result of the communist ideology that services of almost all kinds are unproductive and do not add value. So banking services, hairdressers, computer services, cabdrivers, and so on were excluded from the economic measurement of a country.

4. In the late 1980s only, direct subsidies for food (negative turnover tax) were almost 10 percent of total expenditures. In other words, 7 percent of the net material product was redistributed for these purposes.

5. We could quote other differences between the monobank and both the central and the commercial banks of market economies that were reflected, for example, in the structure of the balance sheet. For technical details, see Garvy (1966).

6. The tradition of non-inflationary growth, at least regarding open inflation, has been already presented. Sargent (1982) gave a historical explanation for it: Czechoslovakia never experienced a period of hyperinflation or even galloping inflation, and the development in the early 1920s is an excellent example of deflationary postwar recovery. The presence of these ideas in the 1980s is an example of this prewar intellectual heritage.

7. One may prove, on empirical evidence, quite different interest rate elasticities of money (credit) demand between these sectors. In previous decades, a firm's demand showed an elasticity near zero. This led to a significant problem with macroeconometric modelling, and models with explicit money measures were rare (see Brada, King, and Schlagenhauf 1981). Usually, only particular parts of the economy were modelled, such as the foreign trade sector or household sector (see Portes and Winter 1978). In fact, only households behaved in this standard manner.

8. There was, on the other hand, significant and rapid comparative decrease in economic performance, measured in U.S. dollars, of gross domestic product per capita. There are several publications that show very wide ranges of estimates depending on the employed methodology. In all cases, the relative decrease as compared with OECD countries is obvious (see Marer 1985; Havlik 1985).

9. The final outcome is not surprising—the overvaluation of macroeconomic data. In reality, we should subtract about 2 to 3 percent of hidden inflation per annum from NMP growth rate. Also, consumer satisfaction declined. It is intuitively understandable that in particular sectors, these defects have displayed different intensities. The estimates of hidden inflation rates in the machinery

sector were completely different from that of construction (25 and 10 percent per year, respectively). Similar examples from the Soviet Union have been presented (Legget 1981).

10. Rates of savings (household savings/disposable income) fluctuated between 2.9–4.4 percent per year in the 1970s and 1980s, which is less than in the United States and OECD countries. In 1989 and 1990, this rate was close to 2 percent, excluding savings abroad and capital investment.

11. There could be an objection that when the aggregate income remains unchanged, due to prudential monetary and fiscal policy, inflation could never evolve. This is not quite true, as there is the possibility of dissaving, which depends on inflationary expectations. Also, additional income can be raised by selling property (land, houses, antiquities, etc.) to foreigners. In the transition period, there can evolve purely statistical problems. For example, new products enter the market, leading to shifts in weights in the price index that could make it non-comparable with previous calculations. Or different goods may have different price elasticities, which could result in further shifts in weights if major relative price changes occur.

12. Minister of Finance Vaclav Klaus, in his keynote address to the annual meeting of the International Monetary Fund in April 1990, said that "sometimes we are not sure whether the current economic situation is in reality an asset or a liability" (Klaus 1990).

13. The entrepreneurial bank (*Zivnostenska banka*) was the most important Czechoslovak bank before World War II. The name of the bank was preserved, in fact, only because it has had the branch and building in London. The investment bank was created in 1949, and up to the middle of the 1950s, it managed the credit rationing for investment. After the takeover of this agenda by the state bank, the investment bank was preserved without any economic reason, since its latter agenda could have easily been managed by any other bank.

14. The growth rate of nominal money supply was set at 3 percent in 1990 due to an expected increase in velocity (10%), decrease of real output by 3 percent, and expected inflation of 15 percent. The equation of exchange expressed in rates of growth ($gM + gV = gP + gQ$) had then the following figures $(3 + 10 = + 16 - 3)$ in 1990, where gM = growth rate of the nominal money, gV = growth of velocity, gP = inflation rate, and gQ = growth rate of real output.

15. It is obvious that those limits are quite different from the limits facing the Polish government. According to polls, inflation of over 40 percent and unemployment over 10 to 15 percent for more than two years seem to be unacceptable in Czechoslovakia. The unemployment target for 1991 was even set at a 5 percent level.

16. To achieve this can be a difficult task. Rising oil prices, cold winters, or bad harvests could create very strong pressures on the stability of the balance of payments. The balance of payments is targeted at the U.S.$2.5 billion deficit in 1991, and the external debt is projected to be about U.S.$12 billion, or 37 percent of the GDP.

17. Similar dangers could be created via devaluation expectations; the public would not save in domestic currency and would hoard foreign exchange and/or deposit it in foreign banks (see Mejstrik 1991).

18. The risk of cost-push inflation has increased with the lifting of controls over private sector wages and prices, which is an important element in the policy to promote the expansion of the private sector. In the short run, the need to control cost-push inflation in a disequilibrium economy may justify the continuation of some form of wage control (for example, setting an indexing rule for an increase in enterprise wage bills) and price control both in the state sectors and in the markets for "necessities." Such a system must, however, be seen as temporary.

19. The old system used at least two kinds of exchange rates, one for commercial transactions and another for tourist purposes. The second one was significantly higher, partly because it served as a "tourist tax" and partly because it reflected the different price levels within the consumer and production sectors. Both exchange rates were unified by the end of 1990.

Chapter 7

The Transformation of the Czechoslovak Economy and Unemployment

Milan Sojka

In the European context, Czechoslovakia had a relatively developed economy before World War II. During the postwar period, as a consequence of implementation of the Soviet type of centrally planned system and the distortion of its foreign trade relations due to its incorporation into the Soviet bloc, Czechoslovakia lost its economic efficiency. Even if Czechoslovakia and Eastern Germany had the most efficient centrally planned economies, relative to the Western European market economies, they now have far lower labor productivity and are technologically backward.

The events of November 1989 at last opened the possibility to implement a democratic political system and to start the process of transition from a centrally planned to a market economy. All over Eastern Europe, efforts to transform the existing centrally planned economies into market ones are growing and becoming stronger. Until now, this transformation process has not been successful, and all the East European countries are facing new unresolved problems.

Apart from the former East Germany, which, after the unification of Germany, has rather special conditions, the problems and risks involved in the process of transition are very similar in all of the East European countries, even if their preconditions and relative stages of development are different.

At the very beginning of the transformation process, Czechoslovakia had the advantages that the disequilibria in the economy were not too great and that it has a relatively skilled and cheap labor force. As a latecomer to the process of transformation, Czechoslovakia can take into account the experiences of Hungary and Poland.

The risks involved in the transformation process are closely connected to its depth and radical nature. The main initial steps in the process include privatization of state enterprises, the development of the private sector, and liberalization of prices and foreign trade. The preliminary requirements of the transformation process reside in a new legal framework leading to a radical change in economic institutions and their mutual relations.

The main threats to the transformation process consist of growing inflationary pressures and unemployment. Czechoslovakia, like all other East European countries, must challenge inflationary pressures from a monetary relic of the past. The long-term open inflation in Czechoslovakia was about 2 percent annually and so-called hidden inflation was estimated at around 3 percent. During the initial period of preparation for the transformation of 1990, the hidden inflation became an open one. Cutting subsidies on food retail prices in July 1990 meant the inflation rate passed 10 percent.

Because of this monetary legacy and existing inflationary pressures, stabilizing macroeconomic policy must be implemented. An effective stabilizing or anti-inflationary macroeconomic policy consists of restrictive monetary and fiscal policies, which have unfavorable effects on unemployment and create recessionary tendencies in the national economy. To be able to face the growing social tensions connected with unemployment, the transformation process must be accompanied by a new government policy concept toward employment and the social safety network.

Perspectives of growing unemployment are narrowly linked not only to the effects of restrictive macroeconomic policy, but also to the turning of hidden into open unemployment, and to the necessary structural changes in the national economy.

FROM HIDDEN TO OPEN UNEMPLOYMENT

One of the supposed advantages of the centrally planned economy was its ability to provide full employment of the labor force. In reality, this claim is rather exaggerated because centrally planned economies generally experienced some low unemployment, of the kind that would be called in a market economy frictional unemployment. This short-term unemployment was not considered to be unemployment; it was not statistically estimated, and it is very difficult to provide any reliable figures on it. This unemployment was very low and very short term because of the legal obligation to have a job. Any person without a job and not living demonstrably on his or her own devices could be prosecuted and sentenced to prison. Exceptions to this obligation included mothers of small children, women living off their husband's incomes, the sick and disabled, and so forth, but the laws sometimes contributed to forced employment.

There was another kind of unemployment in the centrally planned economy that was far more important. This was hidden, covert unemployment, or artificial employment. This is the kind of unemployment we generally find in underdeveloped countries, especially in rural areas, and it is very typical of all centrally planned economies.

The development of centrally planned economies was based on so-called force growth, resulting from central decision making. Without adequate knowledge of the needs of citizens, as no thorough research was undertaken, and without due economic considerations, since real market prices were lacking, the center determined more or less arbitrarily and subjectively production targets for all branches and enterprises in the economy.

The center forced enterprises to minimize inputs and maximize outputs, but it had to rely on the information generated by enterprises. This information was highly unreliable because deliberate distortion was in the interest of enterprises. Enterprises were interested in fulfilling their production targets by the easiest way possible. They tried to persuade the center to minimize the targets assigned to them and to consign additional financial, labor, and other resources. Enterprises actually aimed at maximizing input and minimizing output, and, in fact, the enterprise had an informational advantage in this planning dialogue between the center and enterprises. We will not enter into the details of these problems, but only note that as a consequence of this kind of behavior, the centrally planned economy was highly inefficient.

Enterprises lacked any significant motivation for the efficient use of labor and other resources. In all East European countries, we can find high consumption of labor, materials, energy, and other resources per unit of production in comparison with the developed market economies of the West. The actual utilization of the national labor force in Czechoslovakia has been rather low, even though the employment rate has been high.

The problem of quantitative estimation of this hidden unemployment is very complex. The most reliable method is to compare enterprises in centrally planned economies with corresponding enterprises functioning under the market conditions in Western economies. But it is not easy to consider adequately the impact of the existing technological gap between East European and Western economies.

Some estimates for the Czechoslovak economy show the lower limit of hidden unemployment to be above 6 percent of the labor force. Other studies of Czechoslovak, Polish, and Hungarian enterprises tried to show that the hidden unemployment could be enormous, sometimes up to 25 percent of the working population. We can very reasonably estimate that around 10% of labor force is artificially employed in Czechoslovakia.

The process of transformation aims at creating new competitive conditions and hard budget constraints for enterprises, so that the enterprises will not be allowed to drain government budget resources. As a result, the enterprises will not be able to keep all the artificially employed persons. As the process of privatization or "destatization" of the economy progresses and competitive behavior prevails, the motivation to maximize profits and minimize labor and other costs, and to maximize the rate of utilization of labor and other resources, will dominate in the behavior of enterprises. This process will eventually lead to the conversion of hidden unemployment into open unemployment.

The deteriorating financial liquidity of enterprises will force them to reduce social overemployment and increase the efficiency of their activities. Restrictive macroeconomic policy can have some positive effects in these processes up to a certain extent. But in this connection, an important question remains as to how far government policy can go with restrictive fiscal and monetary policy. If certain limits are crossed, there will be many bankrupt enterprises and recession, with massive involuntary unemployment.

STRUCTURAL UNEMPLOYMENT

The structure of all centrally planned economies was developed according to a forced growth approach, with the allocation of economic resources determined by the center. Central planners have made allocation decisions on the basis of their preferences, where political and power considerations were decisive, and without due consideration to economic efficiency.

Without free markets and under the conditions of centralized price determination, there was, in fact, no way to adequately measure the economic efficiency of resource allocation. A reliable base for calculating marginal efficiency of investment and comparing investment alternatives was absent. The decisions of central planners were biased politically and were rather subjective or voluntary. These decisions somehow took into account the interests and conditions of different industrial branches and enterprises, but there was no functional mechanism for taking into account consumer preferences. In fact, enterprises were motivated to fulfill assigned targets and not to satisfy needs of consumers. Moreover, the structure of production in centrally planned economies evolved almost fully without any consideration of the conditions in world markets and existing tendencies in the development of the international division of labor.

Like the other Eastern European countries, Czechoslovakia now has a very rigid economic structure with a strong, pre-established investment drift, technological backwardness, and low allocative efficiency of economic resources. There is a considerable gap between the structure of supply and demand. This gap grew during the last decades and it manifested itself in rapidly increasing inventories of finished goods on the one side and many shortages on the other. Deteriorating financial liquidity of enterprises is part of this problem as well.

The extent of this misallocation of economic resources in the Czechoslovak national economy is very difficult to assess because of the lack of transparency of a centrally planned economy. It can be evaluated exactly only after the process of transformation is successfully completed; however, the extent of this misallocation is likely to be considerable, as recent developments in post-reunification eastern Germany and Poland show.

Restructuring the Czechoslovak national economy is one of the main tasks in the transformation process. It will be based on a return to market allocation of resources accompanied by an active, pro-market industrial policy. During this process, many existing enterprises must be liquidated and resources must be released from economically unproductive pursuits. This means very rapidly growing structural unemployment, which can especially be a problem in certain regions.

This process must be helped and regulated by government economic policy based on a strong, active, pro-market strategy, and there is no simple scope in this process for Keynesian stimulation of aggregate demand, even if this process should be gradual and under government auspices.

The traditional Keynesian aggregate demand management focuses on deliberate shifting of the actual GNP toward the potential GNP. In our current conditions, we cannot assess with sufficient precision the potential product of our economy, but we can say that it is considerably lower than our current full-capacity product, because a substantial part of current production is not competitive and is not marketable at prices covering existing costs.

An increase in idle production capacities and some increase in unemployment is a necessary consequence of reducing the misallocation of economic resources. An overwhelming part of the unused resources during the transformation process should not be regarded as potential production or as part of existing potential GNP. These idle capacities and unemployment consist predominantly of machinery or labor skills that are of a very uncompetitive nature.

Emerging unemployment will be structural unemployment, but of a somewhat different type than the usual structural unemployment in the developed market economy. The rapid increase in the numbers of structurally unemployed may be impressive and will depend on two main factors. The first factor is the velocity of liquidation of uncompetitive capacities in the state sector, or former state sector, which should undergo reprivatization. In this connection, restrictive macroeconomic policy will as a consequence generate an increase in the velocity of liquidation of these facilities. As a result, the process of reducing the misallocation of resources could be shorter but the corresponding unemployment may be larger. The problem of a socially intolerable rate of unemployment may appear as a possible threat to the transformation process.

The example of East Germany shows that the process of liquidation of excess capacities is very sensitive to foreign trade strategy. The enormous uncompetitiveness of enterprises in former centrally planned economies is a reality. A rapid exposure of these enterprises to world market competition will lead to a breakdown of inner branches and to consequent deindustrialization.

Under such conditions, the liberalization of foreign trade and the introduction of a unique exchange rate must be accompanied by a very selective tariff policy and quantitative limitations of imports. These policies will shelter branches of production that can become competitive in the future. They can as well stagger the process of liquidation of the uncompetitive branches or enterprises, and in this way some threats to the transformation process can be avoided.

A second factor is the potential of the growing private sector to create new jobs. Its rapid development requires legal prerequisites, preferential tax treatment, favorable credit conditions, and so on. From the point of view of the development of unemployment, even minor privatization and restitution are significant, especially in the beginning of the process of transformation. The potential cannot be exaggerated, and some estimates show overall potential to be around 10 percent of labor force. In the service sector, which until now has been rather underdeveloped in comparison with the West European market economies, the job-creating potential is quite important.

As the transformation of existing state-owned enterprises to private ones takes place, large private corporations will be created, which will start to play a decisive role in creating new job opportunities. But it will require some time, probably at least four years, before the big firms are in private hands and can start to play this important role.

THE LABOR MARKET AND UNEMPLOYMENT AT THE INITIAL STAGES OF TRANSFORMATION

The creation of some unemployment is the necessary outcome of the transformation process. It is the result of initiating the process of changes in the national economy under the conditions of inherited overall inefficiency and artificial employment. In the case of Czechoslovakia, there is one demographic factor that will affect the newly emerging unemployment: the population wave of the early 1970s. We not only have the problem of shrinking job opportunities generating unemployment among the formerly employed, but the additional problem of considerable numbers of teenagers entering the national labor force as well. Many of them will be unemployed, with all the adverse effects on the future quality of their skills and their job experience and training.

The process of some reduction of socially inefficient overemployment started in 1989 under the reluctant reform trials of the former communist government. The reduction was in fact rather limited; it concerned state and central planning and the management bureaucracy, and the majority of released labor was able to find other jobs or retire.

During 1990, some increase in unemployment began. Because of political and institutional changes, the reduction of the administrative and bureaucratic apparatus of the Communist Party, government institutions, army, and so on, some 60,000 to 80,000 white-collar workers were released. Job reductions started in state-owned enterprises and in the cooperative sector as well. The overall decrease in job opportunities was estimated at around 100,000, or 1.3 percent of the work force. The majority of these reductions occurred in construction and manufacturing.

During the second half of 1990, there was a large inflow of new graduates from colleges and high schools into the labor force. About one-third of these newcomers were not able to find any jobs until the end of 1990.

We are now at the very outset of the transformation process and the structural changes have up to now only begun. For this reason, at the end of 1990, only a very small rate of unemployment, estimated at around 1 percent of the labor force, emerged. In a market economy, this would certainly be considered full employment. The number is very low, not only in relation to Western market economies but also to other East European countries.

This low rate of unemployment cannot be considered a success, but rather a symptom of the fact that Czechoslovakia is at only the very outset of its transformation and that the process has not progressed far. The bulk of the necessary changes lies ahead, and there are expectations of a rapidly growing rate of unemployment in the early 1990s as all the changes intensify. Table 7.1 shows the current unemployment and other characteristics of the Czechoslovak labor market.

Czechoslovakia now has a labor force of about eight million. Half of the unemployed are blue-collar workers, 11 percent are college graduates, and 32 percent are high school graduates. Sixty percent of all of the unemployed registered by the labor exchanges receive social payment for unemployment. Existing vacancies are usually considered a very important characteristic of labor market conditions. In our situation, these data are not very reliable. Also, as has been explained, the transformation process will lead to the liquidation of inefficient social overemployment and huge structural changes. These processes will inevitably diminish the number of vacancies as well as the number of existing job opportunities.

In 1990, and to a far greater extent in future years, the elimination of existing jobs in the state sector will accelerate and another process of creating new job opportunities in the private sector will emerge as economic strength is acquired. Many internal and external factors will determine the pace of these changes. Taking into account the complexity of these processes, it is very difficult to make an accurate forecast. Some existing estimates of the increase of unemployment in the next three years are shown in Table 7.2.

These figures project rapidly growing numbers of unemployed, and even the lower estimate suggests that social payments will require more than 2 percent of all budget expenditures. Another problem is the social acceptability of a considerably high rate of unemployment and the possibility of social unrest, especially in regions that may be hard hit.

COPING WITH UNEMPLOYMENT IN THE TRANSFORMATION

In the transformation process, there is no possibility of full employment, and no government of an East European country can promise that jobs will be abolished only when new jobs are created in corresponding numbers. The process of transformation will inevitably create considerable rates of

Table 7.1

Czechoslovak Labor Market: The Unemployed, Rate of Unemployment, and Vacancies (December 1990)

	Unemployed	Rate of Unemployment	Vacancies
Czech republic	39,379	0.76	57,616
Slovak republic	37,586	1.76	14,573
Czechoslovakia	76,965	1.00	72,189

Source: Federal Ministry of Social Affairs, CSFR.

Table 7.2

Projections of the Unemployment Rate and Share of Social Payments as Percentage of Budget (1991–1993)

Year	Total Labor Force (in thousands)	Unemployed (in thousands) Var. I	Unemployed (in thousands) Var. II	Rate of Unemployment Var. I	Rate of Unemployment Var. II	Share of Social Payments for Unemployment in the Government Budget
1991	7,938	556	793	7.0	10.0	2.1	3.0
1992	7,993	639	1,198	8.0	15.0	2.3	4.2
1993	8,048	724	1,046	9.0	13.0	2.4	3.5

Source: J. Klacek et al. (1990). *Macroeconomic Analysis* (in Czech). Prague: National Institute of Economics, p. 53.

unemployment, and we cannot escape this. For many inhabitants of East European countries, this may be a great shock, because they have not been used to unemployment and they expect the government to take care of them and to find, or create for them, new jobs. Under these conditions, even the low forecast of unemployment may present a threat to the process of transformation. Our reform scenario includes, for these reasons, a new conception of social security and employment policy measures.

Employment policy should be active, and it should have a strong pro-market orientation. Its aim cannot be the protection of existing jobs; rather, it should promote labor market conditions in which the creation of new jobs is paramount. The goal of the employment policy cannot be full employment, but it should endeavor to the highest employment possible. Of overwhelming importance here is the support of the private sector and the creation of favorable conditions for its development.

The chief line of orientation of employment policy should be active, functional, and efficient job creation, but we cannot escape unemployment in the process of transformation. To alleviate the conditions of the unemployed, the social security net should include the payment of unemployment benefits, for example, at 60 percent of the last net annual wages.

An employment fund and system of labor exchanges were created to cope with the unemployment issues. Labor exchanges were created on a regional basis, and their activities are financed from the government budget. The measures launched should be covered by financial resources released from the employment fund. The main goal of labor exchanges will be the speedy transformation of the unemployed into the employed. Their main activities include the promotion of new job opportunities, implementation of public utility projects, promotion of small-scale entrepreneurial activities, and requalification programs.

The employment fund is designed to finance all the measures related to the employment policy. It will be used to cover the additional costs of new job promotion, including timely provision of functional job opportunities for workers dismissed from their former jobs.

Other government policies are designed to mitigate imbalances in the labor market and to regulate the labor market generally. Increased maternity benefits aim at decreasing the employment of mothers with young children. Other government measures are designed to promote more widespread employment of women in jobs with a reduced working load and to reduce the active participation in the labor force of people of a post-productive age. The supply of labor will be gradually influenced as well by measures designed to extend the period of vocational, graduate, and postgraduate study in preparing young people for their professional careers. These measures can alleviate the evolving disequilibrium in the labor market but cannot effectively eliminate it.

There is only one truly effective long-run strategy to cope with unemployment, and this is based on sustained economic growth. This strategy, however, can be fully applied only after the process of transformation is over. During the process, it can be applied only partially by supporting the development of the private sector and those parts of the public sector whose privatization would be inefficient, such as natural monopolies. A very important role must be played by passive measures aimed at alleviating the lot of the unemployed and thus helping to preserve support for the transformation process.

Chapter 8

Polish Trade Adjustment Under Convertibility

Andrej Kondratowicz and Jan Michalek

This chapter deals with two related phenomena: recent institutional and policy changes in Polish foreign trade, and the resulting adjustment in export-import flows. Of all the systemic changes attempted in Poland in the course of the reform, introducing currency convertibility should be, as we will see, singled out as the most important element.

Trade adjustment has several dimensions, including changes in volume, in composition of commodity groups, and in geographical origination or destination. While focusing on all of the above, we will try not to lose sight of the general picture of reforming the Polish economy. Foreign trade adjustment is therefore seen as but one element of a radical overall adjustment program, known as the Balcerowicz Plan (henceforth BP),[1] consisting of two sequential parts: Phase I—stabilization, and Phase II—structural change.

CHALLENGES OF THE 1980s AND THE RESPONSES

The necessity of attempting a radical economic reform stemmed from the deep and worsening disequilibrium characterizing the Polish economy of the late 1980s. Like all other CPEs, the Polish economy was haunted by numerous incurable inefficiencies manifesting themselves at both the macro and micro levels. The notorious failure to achieve allocative, as well as productive, efficiency led to repeated attempts at reforming the economic mechanism. The repeating sequence of embarking on, and retreating from, a "decentralization" reform, which characterizes all CPEs since the 1950s, has been well documented and analyzed in the literature.[2]

The half-hearted attempts brought only meager results. Cosmetic changes did not alter the wasteful character of the system. Only by over-exploiting accessible resources of all kinds was the system able to function largely unthreatened until the late 1970s.

The beginning of the 1980s was marked by accumulating disequilibria of exceptional depth. A piecemeal approach was tried again but was to little or no avail. By the late 1980s, the crisis was spreading quickly and steadily, while the internal and external resources that in the past decades had served as a substitute for genuine reform seemed to be finally exhausted.

In the period from 1980 to 1989, economic liberalization quickened substantially and was especially visible in the area of foreign trade and its financing mechanisms. But the changes came too late and were too slow to produce any significant improvements in economic performance. A change of economic regime seemed to be the only solution at the end of 1989. At that moment, Poland was politically ready to undertake it.

Before we analyze the general goals and structure of the BP, let us look at some numbers characterizing the situation in the second half of the 1980s. With regard to the internal equilibrium, between 1983 and 1988 the yearly growth rate of GDP was approximately between 4 percent and 5.5 percent (with the single exception of 1987, when it was only 1.8 percent). Signs of stagnation came in 1989: GDP slowed to zero growth. This was a result of a downward trend in the state-owned industrial sector, where output decreased by 3.4 percent in constant prices, and an 11 to 12 percent increase in the private sector.[3]

Employment in the former declined by 4.5%. There was no official unemployment, although numerous state enterprises were believed to be systematically grossly overstaffed. Performance of the economy may be better assessed if we add that the 1989 GDP was still below its peak level of 1978 (GDP declined between 1979 and 1982).

The inflation price index measured by the Consumer Price Index (CPI) was, in the period 1983 to 1986, between 114.8 and 121.7. In 1987, the index was 131.1; in 1988, 173.9; in 1989, 739.6. In 1988, the central budget deficit was 269.2 billion *zloty*, that is, about 4.3 percent of the budget expenditures. In the last quarter of 1989, the Polish parliament introduced a ceiling on the central budget deficit of 5,237.3 billion *zloty*, about 30 percent of the budget expenditure.

Knowing the general condition of the Polish economy, let us look at the external equilibrium. Until 1956, the economies of Eastern Europe remained autarkic for ideological reasons. Surprisingly, even after those restrictions had long been gone, Poland—despite its political emancipation—remained as autarkic as before. The share of exports in GDP was throughout the 1980s in the neighborhood of 20 percent. Exports per capita looked much worse, only slightly exceeding U.S.$300, which placed the country at the very end of the list of European nations.[4] Poland's share in world trade has been going down, averaging about 0.4 percent to 0.5 percent during the 1980s.

The country's foreign trade was administratively divided into two payment areas: Area I concerned trade with Comecon in non-convertible currencies, and Area II was in convertible currencies. As far as Area II is concerned, beginning in 1982, Poland had a trade surplus in the range of one to one and a half billion dollars. In 1988, the surplus, in hard currency, amounted to U.S.$920 million, falling to an eight-year low of U.S.$126 million in 1989. All other elements of the current account balance deteriorated as well, showing a deficit of nearly two billion dollars (compared with U.S.$563 million in 1988). In December 1989, net Polish indebtedness in convertible currencies was U.S.$39.9 billion.

Trade with Area I countries was in balance in 1987. In 1988, it showed a surplus of 496 million transfer roubles (rbt), which doubled to 987 million rbt in 1989. This growth was caused by a 6 percent fall in Polish imports, which was largely due to the Soviet decrease in the supply of fuels and energy theoretically guaranteed under the Comecon umbrella. As a result, Poland had to look for alternative, generally more expensive sources of energy, incurring losses. Despite the large trade surplus, Polish net debt in roubles vis-à-vis Comecon partners remained high, at 5.3 billion rbt.

The overall picture of Polish foreign trade and finance was indeed gloomy, and 1989 showed a marked deterioration of the situation. Liberalization efforts that started in 1987 had to be acknowledged as a fiasco. At the end of 1989, those unanswered challenges were met by the radical proposals contained in the BP.

Phase I of the BP had two broad objectives. The first was to stabilize an economy plagued by hyperinflation and large budget deficits. The second was to start building a skeleton of market institutions, hoping to stimulate competition, with all of its beneficial spillover effects. As various elements of the reform progress, a full-fledged market economy is expected to develop gradually, paving the way to more profound structural changes and economic growth in Phase II.

The goals of the initial phase could not be achieved without paying due attention to rectifying the external disequilibria. These stem directly from the saving-investment identity:

(1) Budget deficit = (private saving - private investment) + (current account deficit)

Equation (2) below gives the way to finance the public sector deficit[5]:

(2) Budget deficit = money printing + (foreign reserve use + foreign borrowing) + domestic borrowing

It follows from Equation (2) that, given the stated goals of eliminating budget deficits (LHS) and curbing high inflation (RHS-money printing) in a situation of low credit-worthiness in Poland (RHS-foreign borrowing), the program's success largely depends on foreign reserve use and domestic borrowing possibilities (both terms of RHS). The use of foreign reserves will in turn depend on the Polish current account position, including the trade balance, and the cooperation of international agencies and countries in providing special stabilization funds. Domestic borrowing possibilities are in part connected with successful "de-dollarization" of the Polish economy and the creation of a climate conducive to increased investment in securities denominated in the local currency. These two features seem to require introducing at least partial convertibility and maintaining a realistic exchange rate.

In sum, foreign trade mechanisms and policies, as well as those pertaining to the foreign exchange sphere, should constitute an integral part of the comprehensive reform package. It comes therefore as no surprise that the BP puts heavy emphasis on "opening up the Polish economy."[6]

Reform of the Polish foreign trade mechanism was to accomplish two goals. First, it was to increase the magnitude of export and import flows—both in absolute terms as well as in the proportion to GDP. Under the old regime, the emphasis had always been on increasing exports and creating a trade surplus. This was seen as the way to finance imports of producer and consumer goods that could not be manufactured domestically, mostly due to technological difficulties. An important point was that imports permitted fighting bottlenecks in domestic production. Less conspicuous but also important was the motive of realizing economies of scale, or simply finding outlets for domestically produced goods (mostly machinery exported to the former Soviet Union).

The second reason was much more important, although at the same time much less understood and grossly underestimated. It was to expose the domestic economy to the price structure prevailing in world markets (i.e., in countries characterized by high economic efficiency). It meant overall rationalization of the allocation of resources in macro and micro perspectives.

For a long time it was believed that the first goal—increasing trade flows—could be achieved within the general framework of the planned economy. In that belief, the institutional and policy liberalization was stepped up in the period 1987 to 1989—as we know, to little avail. Nevertheless, many economists advocated a piecemeal reform, maintaining that setting a realistic exchange rate and introducing convertibility would only destabilize the very fragile foreign trade situation, wreaking havoc on the whole troubled economy. The single gain of squeezing out more exports seemed not worth risking everything.

One would be seriously tempted to share that view, if not for the second goal of foreign trade, the realignment of the domestic price structure. And here the only road was through convertibility and realistic exchange rates. Since the price-led resource-allocation mechanism lies at the heart of the market-oriented reform, it became obvious that those measures should become the centerpieces of the BP. In that environment, other institutional and policy changes, specifically affecting foreign trade, made much more sense.

In discussing the role convertibility and the exchange rate play in the process of creating a market environment, one should not forget their role in stabilization efforts, especially in combating hyperinflation. Here the fixed (pegged) exchange rate was assigned a pivotal role of a nominal stabilizing anchor—the money wage. Since money wages are only partially indexed, this nominal anchor possesses some flexibility. The stabilization program also includes two real anchors: the real money supply and the real interest rate. The analysis of the exact working of all four interrelated anchors, as well as the speed and sequence of introducing the stabilization measures, goes beyond the scope of this chapter.[7]

REFORMING FOREIGN TRADE INSTITUTIONS AND POLICIES

Liberalization of the Polish trade system began back in 1987. The primary objective of the government was to open the domestic economy and gradually dismantle a monopoly that the state enjoyed in foreign trade operations. In fact, the number of companies having license to trade grew to some 3,000 in 1989, but the turnover was still dominated (84% of total exports, and 91% of imports) by 16 large state-owned foreign trade organizations and 32 companies whose majority stake belonged to the state.

Since January 1990, under the Balcerowicz Plan, liberalization has accelerated. Now, all economic units, regardless of their ownership status, are free to export and import. The previous licenses issued for trading remain necessary only in a few exceptional cases.[8] At the same time, the government introduced some transitional, non-discriminatory non-tariff measures. Initially, export quotas covered 22 products that were in short supply on the domestic market in previous years, but since April 1990, there have been only three items on the list. For the same reason, export licenses for another 22 goods (17 at the end of 1990) were applied. This list covers some raw materials, intermediate products, fertilizers, and a few agricultural products.[9] Apart from these interim (in principle) measures, there are also export quotas resulting from external restrictions imposed by some OECD countries, limiting their imports of textiles and clothing, footwear, and steel products.

On the import side, the restrictions are even less important. Licenses are still required in the case of a few strategic products. They had also been required until the end of 1990 to import from the Comecon countries, when the trade was denominated in inconvertible currencies. In addition, the new Customs Law of December 1989 created the possibility to establish duty-free zones and duty-free warehouses.[10] In the latter, Polish enterprises can process and store goods for up to three years without being liable for customs duties.

* * *

The most profound changes occurred in the area of the foreign exchange regime.[11] The two pivotal points of the new system are internal convertibility for current account transactions, and a unified, fixed exchange rate (expressed in terms of the U.S. dollars).

This means that each and every domestic physical or legal person (including partly or wholly foreign-owned enterprises having their main offices in Poland) can, without limitation, purchase foreign exchange, provided it is to cover the costs of a current account (i.e., non-capital) transaction. The currency is purchased at the current exchange rate announced by the National Bank of Poland (NBP), which was initially set for an unspecified period of time at 9,500 *zloty* per U.S. dollar.[12]

Moreover, all transactions in goods and services must be denominated and effectuated in foreign currencies: the Polish *zloty* must not enter into international circulation. Transactions with Comecon countries, except for a small margin, continued to be carried out according to old rules until the end of 1990. Starting on January 1, 1991, the transfer rouble was abandoned altogether and replaced by hard currencies. Nevertheless, many important details of payments with particular Comecon partners have not yet been worked out, leaving room for uncertainty.[13]

As soon as the Comecon countries introduce convertibility for their enterprises[14] or at least establish well-defined foreign currency distribution systems within their national economies, the general payment rules (as spelled out in the Polish Exchange Law) will also apply to the transactions with them. Those general rules are:

1. The Polish exporter sets the contract price in foreign exchange and has to require the payment within a maximum of three months; it is not allowed to extend merchant credit. Then, the money due must be transferred to Poland within a maximum of two months (which seems to be a device to prevent the enterprises from playing on leads and lags).

2. The exporter must surrender (sell) the foreign exchange received to a qualified Polish bank in full.

3. The qualified banks resell the foreign exchange to the National Bank of Poland.

4. The NBP is obliged to sell foreign exchange to the qualified banks (so-called foreign exchange banks) on their demand.

5. The foreign exchange banks are obliged to resell foreign exchange to domestic persons (residents) without any limitation or additional permits and licenses as long as the money is to cover the aforementioned current account titles.

Let us stress the fact that internal convertibility means not only the unlimited possibility of acquiring foreign exchange by a Polish importer, but also an obligation to do so. Collecting payment in Polish *zloty* is forbidden. Internal convertibility, therefore, is essentially convertibility for domestic importers. Availability of foreign currency to importers on demand creates a kind of microeconomic illusion or simulation of convertibility. The important point is, nevertheless, that this simulated convertibility has so far been enough to favorably alter the previous autarkic decision-making behavior of Polish microeconomic agents. The general mechanism of export and import decisions is the same as it would have been under full (internal and external) convertibility on current account.[15]

Since the initial exchange rate had to be fixed administratively, there was a widespread fear of a large trade deficit and a run on foreign exchange, resulting in the dramatic depletion of hard currency reserves. In light of decades of excess demand for foreign exchange, those fears were not unfounded. In order to be able to defend convertibility, Poland gathered substantial monetary reserves—partly in the form of special stabilization funds contributed by industrial countries.[16]

As we will see in the next section, the Polish trade balance has been showing a record surplus, there was no run on foreign exchange, and the foreign reserves position has not deteriorated. This seems to support the thesis that convertibility—even in its limited or "simulated" version—has favorably affected the export-import decision making on the micro level, making the firms and households react to price signals from international markets.[17]

The institutional changes have been reinforced by a number of important policy switches, although their importance is not to be overestimated as yet.

In 1990, domestic prices reached the structure and level that enabled them to perform a market function. Thus, the elimination of the state-operated foreign trade compensatory account, which was used to adjust the world prices to the domestic level, was possible. On the export side, the majority of non-tariff measures (such as income and turnover tax exemptions, bonuses from the fund of the minister for Foreign Economic Relations, or direct subsidies), which previously were necessary because of the "submarginal" official exchange rate level, now became obsolete. The major financial measures still in use consist of refunding to the exporters of some fiscal fees charged on inputs incorporated in products being exported.[18] Also, the Export Development Fund provides the financial means to projects oriented at restructuring production and subsidizes forms of exporting (at contractual prices fixed by the state) to East European countries.

On the import side, changes are more important. Free access to convertible currencies at a uniform, stable exchange rate eliminated the rationale for maintaining numerous special arrangements, especially the so-called currency retention accounts (RODs) which were gradually abandoned in the course of 1990.[19] In this new environment, customs duties have a genuine impact on the domestic price level of the imported products and thus have become the main instrument of import regulation.

The new Customs Law, in force since January 1990, is compatible with international standards. The tariff nomenclature is based on the Harmonized Commodity Description and Coding System. The customs valuation and anti-dumping procedures are also in line with the General Agreement on Tariffs and Trade (GATT) articles. The average level of tariff rates is 8.9 percent ad valorem. The duties on the most-favored-nation basis are applied to all GATT and Comecon members (on a reciprocal basis). Special preferences are granted to the developing countries. Tropical products and goods from the least developing countries are imported duty-free.

Thus, tariffs have become the main element of trade policy. In 1990, the government, acting under pressure of various lobbies, liberalized imports. The most visible example was a substantial reduction in tariffs levied on inputs for agricultural production. In January 1990, the customs duties applied to fertilizers and agricultural machinery were reduced. And since April 1990, imports of agricultural machines and pesticides have been duty-free. These changes were due to the declining demand for food in the domestic market.

THE NEW EXTERNAL EQUILIBRIUM

Before we go to the specifics of the trade-related issues, let us have a brief look at the internal equilibrium position after one year from the beginning of the reform.

Recessionary tendencies were still strong. For example, the economy witnessed decreasing industrial output (only 77% of the previous year's level). Although the private industrial sector recorded an 8 percent growth, its share was still too small to influence the overall picture.

Unemployment, non-existent in 1989, appeared in January 1990 and grew steadily throughout the year. On December 31, 1990, there were 1.1 million registered unemployed. The unemployment rate reached 6.1 percent and was still growing in January 1991. Nevertheless, the increase has slowed each month since July, when it peaked at 131,000 (compared with a jump of 35,000 in December).

Two important points are to be made in that connection. First, the overall drop in domestic product was deeper than that in employment, pointing to decreasing labor productivity. Second, in comparison with other countries, it would be naive to expect the Polish natural rate of unemployment to be about 6 to 7 percent; it may be twice as much, or higher.

Surprisingly, the central budget showed a surplus throughout 1990. At the end of November 1990, the surplus was 4.4 billion *zloty* (i.e., almost 3.9% of the budgetary outlays), exerting unnecessary deflationary pressure on the economy.

After two months of rampant inflation (80% in January and 23% in February), the economy showed some promising signs: Between March and December, inflation, as measured by the CPI, was contained between 1.8 percent and 7.5 percent per month.

Adjustment in Polish Trade Flows

Let us analyze the impact of the Balcerowicz reforms on the external equilibrium and the structure of foreign trade, data for which are presented in Table 8.1. In that context a word of caution is due. It may be reasonably maintained that as of January 1991, major institutional reforms in foreign trade had already been completed and that future changes will stem mostly from fine-tuning of the relevant policy parameters. Nevertheless, one should keep in mind the time lags between the changes introduced in 1990 and their results, as reflected in the magnitude and structure of trade flows. These will not be seen in full until two or three years elapse. Thus, the following trade adjustment process should be viewed as interim and preliminary only.

The first and most obvious change in comparison with 1989 was a large trade surplus, which arose both in relation to industrialized countries (U.S.$3798 million, compared with only U.S.$240 million in 1989)[20] and with East European countries (4.787 billion rbt compared with 978 million rbt a year earlier). These figures are not very impressive by industrialized countries' standards, but they are truly significant for the Polish economy. Exports were almost half again higher than imports (44.6% with the industrialized nations and 42.8% with the East European countries).

This was due to several causes. Imports decreased substantially: from the West they were lower by 24 percent, and from Eastern Europe, by 40.4 percent. This happened despite the liberalization of import policy. The main explanation is the sharp reduction of real aggregate demand (absorption), as a consequence of the restrictive monetary and fiscal policy of the Mazowiecki government. It must be remembered that in this period, industrial production of state-owned enterprises decreased by some 30 percent. An even larger decrease of imports from East European countries should be attributed mainly to the rapidly shrinking Soviet exports, resulting from the dramatic disintegration of the Soviet economy. Unexpectedly low domestic demand forced Polish producers to increase their convertible currency exports by 24.6 percent during the first three quarters of 1990 and by almost 40 percent during the whole year. All this occurred in the environment of a high rate of domestic inflation coupled with a firmly fixed exchange rate.[21] The exports to East European countries decreased by 8.5 percent, but this figure is unexpectedly small if we take into consideration that for Polish enterprises, the rouble was devalued against the dollar in January 1990, and that the Polish government intro-

Table 8.1
Polish Foreign Trade by Branch and Currency Area
(January through September 1989)

Non-convertible Currency Area in Millions RBT

Specification	Exports 1990	I-IX 1989 = 100	Imports in I-IX 1990	I-IX 1989 = 100
Electro-eng. ind.	4683.3	61.6	2100.7	61.6
Fuels & power	661.7	95.0	1210.1	58.6
Metallurgical ind.	175.9	68.7	329.6	62.2
Chemical ind.	841.2	96.7	268.8	51.5
Light ind.	153.0	46.7	150.9	67.3
Food ind.	103.3	89.6	78.7	42.0
Agricultural prod.	81.9	64.2	32.8	180.8
Total	7600.2	91.5	4396.5	59.6

Convertible Currency Area in $ Millions

Electro-eng. ind.	1833.3	126.9	1806.9	116.5
Fuels & power	831.1	106.7	705.8	194.2
Metallurgical ind.	1320.7	131.3	317.0	65.0
Chemical ind.	939.4	137.3	518.1	47.4
Light ind.	516.3	130.8	301.4	65.3
Food ind.	866.3	107.7	301.8	41.0
Agricultural prod.	409.7	131.6	73.1	11.8
Total	7623.7	124.6	4225.1	75.7

Source: Central Statistical Office (OSC), Statistical Information on Economic Situation of Poland (Warsaw, October 1990: 91).

Notes: Values in current prices, imports f.o.b. Average exchange rates: 1 rbt = 2,067 zl; $1 = 9,257 zl.

duced (for six months) a multiple exchange rate system, which discouraged exports to the Soviet Union.[22]

The introduction of internal convertibility and the adjustment of exchange rates has also had an impact on the geographic structure of Polish trade. The share of East European countries in Poland's 1990 turnover (export plus import) shrank when compared with the comparable period of 1989. For example, expressed in 1989 prices, the share of non-convertible exports was 40.8 percent in 1989[23] and 33.9 percent in the first three quarters of 1990. This switch in the geographic structure is much more apparent when we take into consideration current rather than constant prices and exchange rates. Then, the share of Eastern European countries in imports decreases to 18.9 percent, and in exports to 18.2 percent (in the first three quarters of 1990).[24] This is the consequence of a devaluation of the rouble in the exchange rates applied by the NBP. It remains an open question which structure is more realistic. The latter has greater meaning for analyzing the financial situation of enterprises. The former is probably more important at the macroeconomic level.

This switch in geographic composition was particularly visible in imports of two categories of goods. Imports of the electro-engineering industry products from the Eastern European countries decreased by 39.4 percent, while those from industrialized countries increased by 16.5 percent. This phenomenon reflects the preference of Polish enterprises for more expensive but higher quality spare parts and investment goods, especially as the domestic economy is haunted by depression. The same fact can be observed in the purchases of fuels and energy. The imports from Eastern European countries (mainly the Soviet Union) decreased by 41.4 percent, while those expressed in convertible currencies increased by 94.2 percent. This phenomenon reflected Soviet cutbacks in the supplies of crude oil and gasoline to Poland.

The changes on the export side are more in line with general trends. The rate of expansion of exports to the West was substantially lower in the cases of food industry products and of fuels. The most disappointing outcome was a sharp decrease (by 39.4%) of the exports of the electro-engineering industry products to the Eastern European countries. This resulted from the low exchange rate of the rouble and from shrinking investment demand in the Soviet Union. This situation may lead to the bankruptcies of the Polish enterprises traditionally linked with the Soviet market. But in general, with the exception of the latter, the changes in the product structure of Polish trade reflected the supply and demand conditions of the domestic economy.

Macroeconomic Consequences of Reforms

The overall 1990 trade balance, adding up the effects obtained in both currency areas together, came to a stunning equivalent of nearly U.S.$5 billion. In an economy like Poland's, which for decades has unsuccessfully tried to implement policies of export promotion and import substitution, it is hard to grasp the true meaning of this phenomenon. A trade balance surplus has always been considered a success, and it comes as a surprise to see that it may be just another guise for a fundamental macroeconomic disequilibrium. It is a kind of an embarrassment of riches.

It is also sobering to notice that this success has no father: although ex ante the phenomenon seems to fit well the absorption theory of the balance of payments, none of the analysts standing close to the Polish reform had predicted even the approximate magnitude of that surplus. It only points to the fact that modeling a developed market economy is quite different from modeling a stabilization program executed simultaneously with the transition from a centrally planned to market economy.

Moreover, the ensuing situation has some important practical bearings; there is an obvious dark side to this huge surplus. One of the problems is positive in character and has to do with controlling the monetary aggregates and conducting a monetary policy. It might be that the NBP possesses no necessary theoretical expertise or, for that matter, previous experience with sterilization procedures.

Another problem is rather normative in nature. Poland bears a heavy burden of foreign debt, and it is engaged in some delicate procedures with both public and private lenders. In light of such an unusually high surplus it may be difficult to convince some banks about the absolute need for further debt rescheduling, not to mention substantial write-offs.

There might be some other negative macroeconomic consequences of the surplus, but it would be unfair and artificial to argue that it brings only negative effects. After all, the reserves of the NBP have increased substantially, and in the fall of 1990 they became an important stabilizer. They were used to offset the increased prices of imported crude oil during the Iraq crisis, while other Eastern European countries suffered from gasoline and motor oil shortages. In addition, the increased foreign exchange reserves were used as high-powered money to expand domestic credit.[25] After the presidential election, they also helped to increase the maneuvering space of the new government.

Changes in the geographic structure of Polish foreign trade will probably become more evident after 1991, for there is a substantial time lag between the policy changes and their full results. Until 1990, trade among the Comecon countries was regulated by bilateral clearing agreements. The prices stipulated in these agreements were based on the moving five-year average of world prices and remained unchanged during the year. They did not, however, properly reflect the quality differentials, since the low-quality manufactured goods of the Eastern European countries were priced at levels comparable to those of the leading world producers. Thus, there was a hidden premium for exporters of those manufactured goods.

Since January 1991—as a result of Soviet pressure—all trade with the Soviet Union has been denominated in convertible currencies and at prices comparable to current world prices. This means that relative prices of Soviet raw materials (standardized products) will become higher, while the prices of Polish low-quality industrial goods will have to decrease. This short-run deterioration in Polish terms of trade will lead to substantial losses. According to the newest estimates,[26] in 1992 Poland will lose about U.S.$1 billion. Only the necessary process of gradual adaptation of Polish firms to the market economy requirements can, in time, reduce these costs. Possible market-oriented reforms in the Soviet Union and other Eastern European countries would also enhance "normal" trade in the region of Europe.

Because of those changes, the Council of Mutual Economic Assistance will probably be transformed into an informal organization whose main role is to provide the framework for exchange of information and a forum for economic negotiations. Poland, like some other Eastern European countries, has already expressed its wish to be associated with the European Community; its ultimate policy goal, which is impossible to accomplish in the near future, is to become a full EC member.

CONCLUDING REMARKS

In this chapter we have presented the economic and political background of the foreign trade and payments difficulties that Poland grappled with through the late 1980s. Those difficulties were only a part of an acute crisis looming over the entire economy. The foreign trade problems could be solved only in connection with other corrective measures constituting a comprehensive, radical reform package known as the Balcerowicz Plan (BP).

One of the cornerstones of the plan was the introduction of (limited) currency convertibility. On the one hand, it permitted the opening up of the Polish economy, stimulating trade growth and allowing a gradual realignment of the domestic price structure. On the other, via the fixed exchange rate regime, it served as one of the two nominal anchors designed to prevent the economy from sliding back into the abyss of hyperinflation.

Numerous changes in institutional features and policies pertaining to foreign trade were introduced. The major results may be summarized as follows. From the legal point of view, all Polish enterprises now enjoy almost unrestricted access to foreign markets, although the actual process of trade de-monopolization has been rather slow. The convertible currency enables microeconomic rationalization of import and export decisions and creates a powerful (although so far not actively used) macroeconomic policy instrument in the form of the exchange rate. It activates tariffs, which became the main instrument of trade policy. The new Customs Law is compatible with international (GATT) standards.

There appeared, however, several unpleasant complications. The Mazowiecki government had to conduct very tight monetary and fiscal policies. As a consequence, inflation was curbed, but the industrial production of state-owned enterprises decreased by some 30 percent, while unemployment began to rise, reaching 6.5 percent in January 1991. This sharp reduction of domestic absorption limited the demand for imports, and as a result the Polish economy saw a substantial trade surplus. The government did not anticipate such a large surplus (or such a sharp decrease of national product) but was reluctant to actively use the exchange rate policy and revalue. This situation made the struggle against inflation much more difficult. The mounting economic hardships connected with the BP undoubtedly contributed to the fall of the Mazowiecki government after the presidential elections; nevertheless, Balcerowicz himself stayed in his post as finance minister, continuing the reform. Another phenomenon, which is partly exogenous and partly due to the foreign trade reform, is the changing geographical composition of Polish trade flows. The increase in the share of market economies (relative to that of the Comecon) can mainly be attributed to the disintegration of the Soviet economy and the Comecon links. This finally led to the discontinuation of bilateral trade arrangements in the framework of Comecon. Another influence on the changes in geographic structure of trade flows was the devaluation of the rouble vis-à-vis the dollar in the exchange rates used by the NBP. In general, the changes in the product structure of Polish trade properly reflected basic supply and demand relations.

Let us conclude by asking what lessons may be drawn from the Polish experience for other Eastern European countries and the former Soviet Union.

First, even in the newly reformed economy, there is a very strong correlation between internal and external equilibrium. This follows directly from the standard Keynesian analysis, but it was to some extent overlooked by Polish economists and politicians. Thus, the governments of other Eastern European countries attempting to reform their economies should take into consideration the repercussions of tight monetary and fiscal policy for internal equilibrium (drop of industrial production and rise of unemployment) and for the trade surplus. Because of this, the social and political support for economic reforms is a crucial element.

Second, the monetary authorities introducing convertibility should take care not to undervalue the domestic currency. But even if the mistake is made, the central bank should not hesitate to revalue the local currency when the trade surplus becomes pronounced. Otherwise, it will be difficult to curb inflation, and domestic social tensions may provoke serious political problems, damaging the reform.

Third, only radical reforms may change the economic situation in a visible manner. Long-lasting attempts to gradually enhance Polish foreign trade yielded only very limited success. Thus, the introduction of convertibility (not only internal but, in some views, external) is a crucial element for market-oriented reforms designed for the opening up of the economy.

NOTES

1. See, for example, IMF (1990: 57–62).

2. For a classical treatment, see Bornstein (1979b), which gives not only a description but also the logic behind the process.

3. All data are from the Polish Central Statistical Office (CSO), unless stated otherwise.

4. In 1987, the combined value of exports and imports per capita was $612, that is, three times less than in Hungary and six times less than in Bulgaria or East Germany. In 1988, it grew to $692, falling back to $639 in 1989. See, for example, Foreign Trade Research Institute (1990: 10).

5. See Fischer and Easterly (1990).

6. In the following text, our goal is to shed light on the foreign trade issues first. The foreign exchange problems are taken up only insofar as they are connected with the former.

7. For a sketch of analysis, see Pitzner-Joergensen (1990: 6–13).

8. A license is necessary to trade radioactive materials, military equipment, and to render agency or representative services for foreign partners ("Ruling by the Polish Minister for Foreign Economic Relations" 1989).

9. See Piotrowski (1990: Annex 3, 42). These products can be exported only by Polish-owned enterprises.

10. Effective January 1, 1990. See, for example, "Polish Customs Duty Law" (1989).

11. Poprawka do Prawa Dewizowego z dnia 15 lutego 1989 (Amendment to the Foreign Exchange Law of Feb. 15, 1989). See "Amendment to the Polish Foreign Exchange Law" (1989).

12. Despite continuing inflation, it remained at the same level throughout 1990.

13. Especially in the case of trade with the Soviet Union and the Balkan countries. The new trade agreement with the Soviet Union stipulated the continuing possibility of barter transactions for an unspecified interim period.

14. Hungary did it in January 1991, while some questions remained regarding Czechoslovakia. See, for example, Buchanan (1990).

15. Leaving aside the problem of the exchange rate regime and level.

16. To support the exchange rate Polish authorities arranged for a bridge loan from the Bank for International Settlements (BIS) in Basel and the U.S. Treasury, as well as a stabilization fund from a number of industrial countries, amounting to about $1 billion. In addition, the IMF approved a standby arrangement for Poland for up to Special Drawing Rights (SDR) 545 million. See, for example, IMF (1990).

17. One should add, however, that this favorable outcome must be at least in part attributed to the firms' use of their pre-1990 accumulated foreign exchange (ROD) accounts and to an abnormally high increase in inventories (equipment, components, raw materials) bought from abroad at the end of 1989 in anticipation of a dramatic devaluation of the *zloty*, which occurred on January 1, 1990.

18. Exports are fully exempt from the turnover tax, and exporters are eligible for a refund of indirect turnover taxes incorporated in the prices of some intermediate goods.

19. Under the previous regime, exporters were obliged to resell a part of their currency earnings to the state bank, while keeping the rest on these retention accounts.

20. Using the IMF guidelines, it was U.S.$126 million.

21. Many economists thought, in the beginning of 1990, that the exchange rate was too low (i.e., the *zloty* price of dollars was too low), and that it would not be stable for more than a three-month "advertised" period.

22. From April to September 1990, the exchange rate for transactions not covered by bilateral agreements was 1 rbt = 1,000 *zloty*, while the standard rate was 1 rbt = 2,100 *zloty*.

23. See Foreign Trade Research Institute (1990: 19, Table 1.4).

24. Calculations are based on the data from Table 8.1 (with current exchange rates).

25. In mid-December 1990, Polish banks started offering dollar-denominated credits, charging rates comparable to those of Western banks.

26. The estimates were made in October 1990 by the Polish Foreign Trade Research Institute in collaboration with World Bank experts (private communication).

Part III

Microeconomic Issues

Chapter 9

Small Is Also Beautiful in the East: The Boom of Small Ventures in Hungary

Katalin Szabo

In the 1980s, Hungary shed the limits of its large organizations in an explosion of small-scale activity. New ventures and new forms of proprietary rights were created. Most of them were not totally new constructions, but rather adaptations of the usual forms found in the more developed economies, or reincarnations of organizations existing in Hungary before nationalization (e.g., share companies). The structure of proprietary rights became almost unrecognizable with the proliferation of new organizations. The developments have corroborated the statement of a famous Hungarian writer known for his irony: "The nation came to its senses" (Esterhazy 1979).

The small-venture[1] sector has proved to be the most dynamic in this wave of transformation. In this short study, we will try to describe the characteristics of Hungarian small ventures and their place in the Hungarian economy.

OPPRESSION AND REVIVAL

In Hungary, as in the other Eastern European countries, small enterprises were simply erased from the map of the economy by socialism. In 1940, about 45 percent of the total employed in industry worked in this sector (Berent and Ranki 1972). In 1950, small industry employed only 5.3 percent, and in 1980 not more than 0.1 percent, as a result of a government policy of systematic repression of small enterprises. The elimination of small business is documented in Table 9.1.

Table 9.1
Industrial Enterprises Employing Fewer than 100 Persons Between 1950 and 1980

Year	Number of Companies	Number of Employees	Percent of Small Companies in all Industry	Percent of Employees at Small Companies in all Industry
1950	710	25,800	49.7	5.3
1955	425	20,600	31.4	3.1
1960	231	12,700	18.2	1.5
1965	100	5,600	14.0	0.6
1970	76	3,400	10.1	0.4
1975	66	2,300	9.1	0.2
1980	45	1.6	6.9	0.1

Source: Péter Pukli, *A Kisvállakoz Helyzete, Múködési Feltételei, További Fejlódési Lehetóségei Magyarországon* (The Small Ventures: Place, Working Conditions, Further Possibilities of Development in Hungary). Budapest: Hungarian Central Statistical Office, 1990.

This reduction occurred in non-industrial economic firms as both services and retail trade were nationalized. All economic units, from the one-man hairdresser's shop to the grocery at the corner, were eliminated. Moreover, the multiple-stage collectivization of agriculture made the big-company structure pervasive for the whole economy.

Hungary—not for the first time in its history—left the main way of world economic development. In Hungary, the structure of the companies and proprietary rights became a "concrete block"[2] —a homogeneous ensemble of some thousands of big companies incapable of any economic flexibility. The official Hungarian economy was even more concentrated than the Soviet or other socialist economies.

This tendency in the Hungarian economy was slightly modified in the 1970s by some limited promotion of small entrepreneurship. The government officially favored large organizations but permitted small organizations outside normal official channels. As a result, the capitalist attitude appeared more and more frequently in the Hungarian economy (Szelényi 1990; Szelényi and Manchin 1988). Data from June 1986 show that about 1,500,000 families were engaged in small-firm production. In addition, 4,448,000 persons were connected to the small-sized family enterprises that constituted about half of the Hungarian population (Szabó and Csicsák 1990: 15). This was unique among Eastern European socialist countries.

After the Hungarian reforms of 1968, individual providers appeared in economic life. In addition, in the collectivized agriculture sector, new, relatively independent forms were established. These were the so-called auxiliary workshops (entrepreneurships). The total number of corporations slightly increased as well.

This promotion of smaller-scale production—realized behind the scenes—had a decisive importance over further developments. Small ventures emerged through the cracks of the concrete walls of the state and cooperative property, producing a dynamic sector of the economy even in adverse circumstances. Participants of the Hungarian economy gained their first experiences of a market economy, though they were often oppressed, suspected, and surrounded by thousands of limits. They accumulated their entrepreneurial knowledge and exercised their spirit of innovation in these rudimentary enterprises. Due to these dynamic enterprises, the country was spared the most difficult forms of shortages. This entrepreneurial strata, working within restrictions, forced the state and the cooperative sphere to change. Hungary, unlike the Soviet Union or Bulgaria, spoke a "market economy language" before the revolutions that swept over Eastern Europe. Hungary learned its language through these small and individual organizations.

1982—THE GREAT YEAR OF THE SMALL ENTREPRENEURS

The inefficiency and waste inherent in socialism motivated the government to change its incentives in 1982. At that time, the government permitted many different organizational forms, all designed to improve the motivation of the players to become more efficient. It was the year of change. Although not all opportunities were given to the small enterprises, in 1982 many barriers and prohibitions were removed. The number and the performance of the small entrepreneurs increased dynamically (see Tables 9.2, 9.3, 9.4, and 9.5).

In addition to the traditional forms (widespread in the more developed countries as well), new organizational forms have been created. Such a new form was the economic work group. The economic work group (GMK) is a corporate venture of two to thirty members who themselves provide production and services. The economic work group was permit-

Table 9.2
Number of Incorporated Companies

Designation	Dec. 31 1988	Dec. 31 1989	June 30 1990	Sept. 30 1990
Total	10,811	15,235	23,257	26,702
From this:				
Enterprises	2,377	2,399	2,408	2,381
Cooperatives	6,880	7,076	7,134	7,141
Economic Corporations	954	5,224	13,158	16,604
From this:				
Share companies	116	307	520	594
Limiteds	451	4,485	12,159	15,561

Source: Péter Pukli. *A Kisvállakoz Helyzete, Működési Feltételei, További Fejlődési Lehetóségei Magyarországon* (The Small Ventures: Place, Working Conditions, Further Possibilities of Development in Hungary). Budapest: Hungarian Central Statistical Office, 1990.

ted only the narrowest range of economic activity: It could engage a maximum of thirty paid employees, it could not trade, and it could only work in the field of industry. (See its growth, including staffing, in Tables 9.6 and 9.7.)

Another particular Hungarian construction is the corporate economic work group, or VGM (see Tables 9.8 and 9.9). This is entrepreneurship within large public companies, a sort of profit center. But in contrast to the usual Western entrepreneurships, they did not become truly independent market organizations (Bakcsi 1987), but worked only by orders of the parent company. The reason for this sort of transformation was that the workshop or division, in the form of the VGM, could demand more money for its products or services from the parent company than could the simple department or workshop within the company earlier. So the VGMs, contrary to the original intention, reduced themselves to workers' brigades working overtime and extracting more money. More details about this form being driven into the background are given in Neumann (1989).

Table 9.3
Number of Incorporated Companies with Fewer than 51 Persons

Designation	Dec. 31 1988	Dec. 31 1989	June 30 1990	Sept. 30 1990
Total	3,588	7,492	14,677	17,298
From this:				
Enterprises	234	234	267	263
Cooperatives	2,268	2,421	2,377	2,378
Economic Corporations	567	4,378	11,531	14,791
From this:				
Share companies	53	117	207	242
Limiteds	352	4,065	11,063	13,282

Source: Péter Pukli. *A Kisvállakoz Helyzete, Működési Feltételei, További Fejlődési Lehetóségei Magyarországon* (The Small Ventures: Place, Working Conditions, Further Possibilities of Development in Hungary). Budapest: Hungarian Central Statistical Office, 1990

The industrial and service cooperative specialized group is another typical Hungarian form. It is like the corporate economic group (VGM) but was formed from parts of big cooperatives. Most of these groups, like the corporate economic work groups, depend completely on the parent organization, working only for it and often being only an overtime brigade. Over time, some of these organizations entered the open market and developed into independent ventures well provided with capital (see Tables 9.10 and 9.11).

In the civil incorporated companies (PJT), private individuals perform common economic activity with a joint liability of all members (see Table 9.12). They have mainly been established in fields (e.g., in the trade) where economic work groups could not work.[3]

In addition, larger organizations have spun off independent units that provided services to the parent. Examples include packaging, publicity, computer service, and so on. Often, the parent firm would purchase shares in the new firm.

Table 9.4
Number of Crafts Workers

	Craftsmen Working			
Year	In Main Occupation	As Retired	In Secondary Occupation	Total
1981	68,900	12,200	30,900	112,000
1982	73,100	12,900	35,400	121,400
1983	76,500	14,300	41,000	131,800
1984	76,100	15,600	47,200	138,900
1984	77,300	17,100	51,200	145,600
1986	78,300	17,800	54,600	150,700
1987	83,400	18,000	53,200	154,600
1988	90,300	18,900	53,000	162,200
1989	100,400	20,000	54,400	174,800

Source: Péter Pukli. *A Kisvállakoz Helyzete, Működési Feltételei, További Fejlődési Lehetóségei Magyarországon* (The Small Ventures: Place, Working Conditions, Further Possibilities of Development in Hungary). Budapest: Hungarian Central Statistical Office, 1990.

PROLIFERATION OF SMALL FACTORIES IN THE LARGE FIRMS

Western economics is motivated by a search for efficiency. During the forty years of socialism, the economy of Hungary was not so motivated. This fundamental difference meant that its economy evolved in a very different way.

A company in the West is organized to produce products at the lowest possible cost. This means that a factory will be structured such that by specializing, it produces at a large enough scale to capture all economies. Thus, either larger or small outputs would lead to higher costs.

In Hungary, since there was no competition, efficiency was less important. Rather, acquiring assured and high-quality supply was much more important. This led to a proliferation of small-scale factories in highly

Table 9.5
Number of Retailers' Licenses

Year	Individual License	Unlimited Partnership	Total	% Change from Previous Year
1981	--	--	14,883	--
1982	--	--	17,287	16.2
1983	21,034	480	21,514	24.5
1984	24,393	539	24,932	15.9
1984	27,633	708	28,341	13.7
1986	31,254	871	32,125	13.4
1987	33,838	1,261	35,099	9.3
1988	35,817	2,167	37,984	8.2
1989	42,058	1,333	43,628a)	14.9

Sources: Péter Pukli. *A Kisvállakoz Helyzete, Müködési Feltételei, További Fejlödési Lehetóségei Magyarországon* (The Small Ventures: Place, Working Conditions, Further Possibilities of Development in Hungary). Budapest: Hungarian Central Statistical Office, 1990.

diversified companies. By having their own production, they could assure themselves of supply, even if it meant that each factory was too small to be efficient.[4]

In the early 1980s, data from 2,210 plants of 398 Hungarian industrial companies were collected. Forty-three percent of them employed fewer than 100 persons, and 16.5 percent employed under 20 persons. Data show that 56 percent of the industrial employees worked in second activities. Parallel capacities have been created at the different enterprises for these supplementary activities. These activities, organized as independent small ventures, can potentially become marketable (see Neumann 1990).

In 1990, limited liability companies founded by big agricultural and trade cooperatives mushroomed. More detailed information about the process is given in the study of Juhász (1987). Often, the formation of these firms was motivated by the desire of the former cooperative manag-

Table 9.6
Number of Economic Work Groups

Year	Total Industry	Industry Broken Down Into:			Personal Economic Service	Other Branches	Total
		Machinery	Light Industry	Construction Industry			
1982	398	225	80	462	362	497	1,719
1983	1,007	581	198	1,056	839	1,043	3,945
1984	1,814	976	457	1,769	1,378	1,702	6,663
1985	2,566	1,291	763	2,260	1,747	2,117	8,690
1986	3,194	1,554	1,024	2,631	1,986	2,406	10,217
1987	3,427	1,617	1,161	2,678	2,005	2,405	10,515
1988	3,288	1,468	1,239	2,239	1,977	2,376	9,880

Source: Péter Pukli. *A Kisvállakoz Helyzete, Működési Feltételei, További Fejlődési Lehetőségei Magyarországon* (The Small Ventures: Place, Working Conditions, Further Possibilities of Development in Hungary). Budapest: Hungarian Central Statistical Office, 1990.

Table 9.7
Number of Members of Economic Work Groups

Year	Total Industry	Industry Broken Down Into:					
		Machinery	Light Industry	Construction Industry	Personal Economic Service	Other Branches	Total
1982	1,932	1,249	287	3,047	1,856	2,645	9,480
1983	5,174	3,230	797	7,265	4,527	5,734	22,700
1984	9,637	5,569	1,972	12,916	7,923	9,518	39,994
1985	14,036	7,677	3,467	17,213	10,058	11,884	53,191
1986	17,857	9,480	4,734	20,384	11,641	13,633	63,515
1987	19,115	9,820	5,392	20,814	11,773	13,768	65,470
1988	16,111	8,110	4,791	15,384	10,653	12,618	54,766

Source: Péter Pukli. *A Kisvállakoz Helyzete, Működési Feltételei, További Fejlődési Lehetőségei Magyarországon* (The Small Ventures: Place, Working Conditions, Further Possibilities of Development in Hungary). Budapest: Hungarian Central Statistical Office, 1990.

Table 9.8
Number of Corporative Economic Work Groups

Year	Total Industry	Industry Broken Down Into:				Personal Economic Service	Other Branches	Total
		Machinery	Light Industry	Construction Industry	Other Material Activity			
1982	1,328	935	131	768	209	189	72	2,586
1983	4,743	3,395	527	2,009	501	1,066	334	8,653
1984	9,273	6,272	1,266	3,036	977	2,320	780	16,386
1985	11,102	7,364	1,489	3,221	1,198	2,717	947	19,185
1986	11,872	7,775	1,550	3,295	1,289	2,871	1,221	20,548
1987	10,557	7,034	1,268	2,763	1,161	2,707	1,161	18,349
1988	7,353	5,105	781	1,699	812	2,200	1,329	13,393

Source: Péter Pukli. *A Kisvállalkoz Helyzete, Működési Feltételei, További Fejlődési Lehetőségei Magyarországon* (The Small Ventures: Place, Working Conditions, Further Possibilities of Development in Hungary). Budapest: Hungarian Central Statistical Office, 1990.

Table 9.9
Number of Employers of the Corporative Economic Work Groups

Year	Total Industry	Industry Broken Down Into:				Personal Economic Service	Other Branches	Total
		Machinery	Light Industry	Construction Industry	Other Material Activity			
1982	15,500	10,200	1,800	8,000	1,800	1,800	800	27,900
1983	54,700	36,000	7,600	20,400	4,800	10,000	3,300	93,200
1984	113,700	69,200	17,600	31,900	9,700	23,500	9,500	118,300
1985	143,400	84,100	21,400	34,400	12,500	28,800	12,200	231,300
1986	159,200	91,500	22,900	36,200	13,900	31,800	17,500	258,600
1987	143,000	83,900	19,200	31,200	12,900	30,600	17,000	234,700
1988	93,700	58,600	11,300	19,400	8,700	24,700	12,400	158,900

Source: Péter Pukli. *A Kisvállkoz Helyzete, Működési Feltételei, További Fejlődési Lehetőségei Magyarországon* (The Small Ventures: Place, Working Conditions, Further Possibilities of Development in Hungary). Budapest: Hungarian Central Statistical Office, 1990.

Table 9.10
Number of Industrial and Service Cooperative Specialized Groups

| | | Industry Broken Down Into: | | | | | | |
Year	Total Industry	Machinery	Light Industry	Chemical Industry	Building Industry	Personal Economic Service	Other Branches	Total
1982	219	134	40	15	166	37	27	449
1983	705	459	132	44	442	71	66	1,284
1984	1,273	745	327	87	720	119	135	2,247
1985	1,495	878	380	101	746	137	168	2,546
1986	1,597	949	398	108	751	145	193	2,686
1987	1,388	819	335	105	594	133	166	2,281
1988	805	492	179	63	346	127	138	1,416

Source: Péter Pukli. *A Kisvállalkoz Helyzete, Működési Feltételei, További Fejlődési Lehetőségei Magyarországon* (The Small Ventures: Place, Working Conditions, Further Possibilities of Development in Hungary). Budapest: Hungarian Central Statistical Office, 1990.

Table 9.11
Number of Employees in the Industrial and Service Cooperative Specialized Groups

Year	Total Industry	Industry Broken Down Into:				Personal Economic Service	Other Branches	Total
		Machinery	Light Industry	Chemical Industry	Building Industry			
1982	5,400	3,500	700	400	5,500	2,800	2,700	16,400
1983	22,400	15,400	3,600	1,200	17,900	3,300	2,400	46,000
1984	41,700	25,700	9,700	2,700	31,500	4,400	3,100	80,700
1985	53,000	33,700	11,400	3,600	31,000	5,000	3,700	92,700
1986	60,100	37,300	14,200	3,700	30,400	5,900	4,800	101,200
1987	53,400	31,700	13,600	3,700	23,100	5,400	3,800	85,700
1988	26,100	16,300	5,200	1,900	13,900	4,000	2,400	46,400

Source: Péter Pukli. *A Kisvállakoz Helyzete, Működési Feltételei, További Fejlődési Lehetőségei Magyarországon* (The Small Ventures: Place, Working Conditions, Further Possibilities of Development in Hungary). Budapest: Hungarian Central Statistical Office, 1990.

Table 9.12
Number of Civilian Incorporated Companies

Designation	1982	1983	1984	1985	1986	1987	1988
Trade	54	197	338	561	1,277	1,903	2,946
Other	135	133	135	118	115	173	215
Total	189	330	473	679	1,392	2,076	3,161

Source: Péter Pukli. *A Kisvállakoz Helyzete, Működési Feltételei, További Fejlődési Lehetőségei Magyarországon* (The Small Ventures: Place, Working Conditions, Further Possibilities of Development in Hungary). Budapest: Hungarian Central Statistical Office, 1990.

ers to capture assets of the cooperatives and privatize them. The problem, however, is not privatization itself, but the fact that such new private executives, although in control of the assets, often have very limited entrepreneurial capabilities.

Nevertheless, the majority of the small ventures, in spite of these problems, is prospering. Their biggest problem is a lack of credit, due to the government's anti-inflation policy and a shortage of collaterable assets.

The funds created to help small ventures are very small, clumsy, and bureaucratic. In practice, the small ventures have to run a complicated gauntlet if they want to get money. "Multiply," says the state, but it does little in favor of the small entrepreneurs. Even today, the small ventures can obtain credit only with difficulty. During 1990, in principle, thirteen types of credit were at the entrepreneurs' disposal. But the entrepreneurs feel that credit is available for them only from the Hungarian Venture Development Fund. In addition, they feel disadvantaged by the tax system and under attack by a society educated in the spirit of the egalitarianism.

The policy of small ventures has been based for more than thirty years on the principle of "restrict and let loose," that is, small entrepreneurs sometimes have a relatively free hand and at other times are limited by economic policy. Today, the situation is the same, but instead of administrative measures, taxation is used as a vehicle to restrict their activity.

In spite of these obstacles, some small firms, through their surprisingly spirited development, have grown to the category of intermediate size with significant market shares and extensive international activity.

Such a success story can be found in the Muszertechnika PJT (Precision Technics, a civil incorporated company). The first objective of this incorporated company, founded by two engineers in 1981, was to earn extra money. In 1982—with a small staff—its turnover was 2,500,000 *forints*, and by 1988, it was 2 billion *forints*. Its success can be measured by the fact that the former incorporated company is today a share company. Muszertechnika's share of the Hungarian PC market today is 25 percent. This intermediate company is a Hungarian international enterprise with a market in West Germany. Its chance to enter the U.S. market is also promising. Recently, this successful firm was at the center of public attention. Its joint venture, with the Swedish Ericsson Technic, won the Hungarian telephone contract, beating out several mature Hungarian telecommunication firms. This single activity of developing the Hungarian telephone network may involve as much as 500,000 lines in three years.

A similar success story is Petrenko. A private entrepreneur from Ozd, Janos Petrenko bought a money-losing foundry. He then set about to enhance the plant's productivity. Worker motivation was improved with better management, salary increases, and higher levels of social benefits. In just two months, Petrenko was able to turn the plant around and make a profit. Today, the Petrenko works has plans to expand; it hopes to buy, for cash, one of its suppliers, the OKU steel works. Janos Petrenko commented on the current state of ventures in Hungary: "I think it important that individuals are free to start new ventures. But the entrepreneurs are even now afflicted by financial regulations. I think that the financial authorities have failed because of the high taxes and the obscurity of the regulators" (Hajnoczy 1990).

Today, there are many ideas and plans aimed at supporting beginner entrepreneurs with aids such as firm-incubator offices equipped with telephone and telefax, and with legal, insurance, and export advice. For this sector to reach its potential, though, it will require a more positive policy by the government.

COMPETITIVE ADVANTAGES OF THE SMALL VENTURE

The rapid development of small ventures stands out in an otherwise stagnant, recessionary Hungarian economy. Why, in spite of such limited support, has this Hungarian David triumphed over the large and preferred, state-supported Goliath? Where does its competitive advantages come from?

Smaller firms possess many competitive advantages that have aided them in their battles with the large, state-favored organizations. The single most important advantage is the enhanced profit incentive operating in these firms. This forces them to make decisions more rapidly and efficiently, and to change when situations change. This motivational difference manifests itself in myriad ways.

As the Hungarian economy has rapidly changed, it has created and foreclosed a series of independent markets. Small firms have moved in and out of these changing markets faster than their larger and less energetic huge government competitors.[5] This greater flexibility of small firms has also manifested itself by their changing their legal forms as governmental legislation changes, thus enabling them to take better advantage of the changing rules than can their larger competitors. In addition, the opportunities and freedom offered by these smaller firms allowed them to attract entrepreneurs and managers of a higher educational level than those working in the large government organizations (see Tables 9.13 and 9.14). A final advantage is that small firms have been more innovative in product development and marketing strategies.

As is characteristic in socialist economies, there are still many areas of shortage in the Hungarian economy. These, in turn, create opportunities for small ventures to satisfy these areas of unmet demand, and in the process, to earn high profits due to the lack of effective competition. In addition to targeting these often specialized markets, the poor distribution system within the country has often created temporary geographical markets exploited by smaller firms.

Another area of advantage in this ineffective competition comes from the nature of these small firms' relations with the law. The Hungarian economy is still hobbled by a plethora of governmental regulations. Small firms, given their less prominent position, are often able to circumvent these regulations, where larger firms are forced to abide by them.[6] One result of many of the obstacles placed in the way of smaller firms by the government policy of favoring large organizations may well have been to toughen them up. This conditioning may have helped contribute to the later robustness of these small and vulnerable firms as they faced increasingly effective competition.

DEFORMATION AND CRIMINALIZATION IN THE SMALL BUSINESS

It is difficult to judge Hungarian entrepreneurs—or any East European small entrepreneurship—with Western eyes. The vigorous promotion of the private sector is considered by Western analysts as a sign of the victory of the market economy over the planned economy. Therefore, they are ready to disregard any unfavorable side effects that may be adding to chaotic conditions. Besides the evident competitive advantages of the small ventures, there are significant negative externalities that are harmful to the national economy. In the light of the business culture and business ethics established in the West, the gray areas in business life, the interpretation of legal and illegal transactions, are often incomprehensible. In certain cases we can speak about the criminalization of the ventures.[7]

The extension of the gray economy in connection with the small-enterprise sector often depends on the restrictive measures of the state, the cruel taxation pressure. The small ventures try to avoid this with the help of illegal maneuvers. Small entrepreneurs often perform their work without receipts because then the work is not taxable. It seems absurd to Western spectators that in Hungary, retailers went on strike against the obligation

Table 9.13
Structure of Entrepreneurs and Earners by Age (in percentages)

Designation	29 and Younger	30-34	35-39	40-44	45-49	50-54	60 and Older
Entrepreneurs	9.9	18.4	22.8	19.9	13.6	12.7	2.6
Earners	27.8	16.9	14.9	13.8	11.2	14.6	0.7

Source: Péter Pukli, *A Kisvállalkoz Helyzete, Müködési Feltételei, További Fejlödési Lehetöségei Magyarországon* (The Small Ventures: Place, Working Conditions, Further Possibilities of Development in Hungary). Budapest: Hungarian Central Statistical Office, 1990.

Table 9.14
Structure of Entrepreneurs and Earners by Education (in percentages)

Designation	Eight Grades or Less	Vocational Sec. School	High School Graduation	High School Graduation and Specialization	College or University	Total
Entrepreneurs	9.1	26.3	24.6	20.4	19.6	100
Earners	36.8	19.3	29.9	--	14.0	100

Source: Péter Pukli. *A Kisvállalkoz Helyzete, Működési Feltételei, További Fejlődési Lehetőségei Magyarországon* (The Small Ventures: Place, Working Conditions, Further Possibilities of Development in Hungary). Budapest: Hungarian Central Statistical Office, 1990.

to give receipts, which is a requirement that is taken for granted in the more developed countries.

It often happens that small entrepreneurs give back their craftsman or retailing licenses and—avoiding the tax offices—perform the same operations illegally. It is characteristic, in particular in tourism and in the catering trade, that the small entrepreneur illegally gets foreign exchange revenue and evades state control. He or she often avoids customs rules and the rules of employment, for example, having employees without paying tax or social insurance for them. When receiving orders, small entrepreneurs often bribe the employees of public enterprises to get the work at unrealistically high prices. Admittedly, all these disorders are of minor importance in comparison with the mobilizing role of the small ventures in the economy.

CONTRIBUTION OF SMALL VENTURES TO THE NATIONAL ECONOMIC PERFORMANCE

The economic growth of Hungary in the stagnant 1980s was solely due to small ventures.[8] The share of non-agricultural small ventures in GDP was 9.3 percent in 1988. In 1988, 6.6 percent of the earners had found their living in these small firms. These data note a tripling of the importance of the sector in the 1980s from 3 and 2.2 percent, respectively, in 1981.

If we include the activity of rural small-scale producers in the sector of small ventures, the performance of the sector would be even more important. The importance of the agricultural mini-firms (household farms) is shown by the fact that the value-added produced by them amounts to half of the value-added produced by the other parts of agriculture. Taking into consideration the mini-ventures working in agriculture as well, the GDP produced by the small ventures surpasses 15 percent of the total GDP. The contribution of the small ventures to the GDP is shown in Tables 9.15 and 9.16.

In 1989, a new law for small ventures was launched. In 1989, the number of corporations (enterprises, cooperatives, small cooperatives, joint stock companies) increased by 41 percent, or 4,358 units, and in the first half of 1990 by 50 percent, or 8,022 units. Within these figures, the number of organizations with fewer than fifty persons doubled from 3,751 to 7,175 units. Also, one-sixth of the new ventures founded in 1990 were with the participation of foreign capital.

Table 9.15
The Role of Small Ventures in GDP Production

| | Small Ventures: | | Large Companies: |
Year	Proportion (percent)	Growth of Volume (percent)	Growth of Volume (percent)
1981	4.8	--	--
1981	5.4	16.8	1.4
1983	8.2	52.7	-1.5
1984	10.4	29.7	-0.6
1985	11.6	11.7	-1.9
1986	13.7	18.4	-1.5
1987	14.6	12.5	4.0
1988	15.2	-0.3	-4.7

Source: Péter Pukli. *A Kisvállakoz Helyzete, Működési Feltételei, További Fejlődési Lehetőségei Magyarországon* (The Small Ventures: Place, Working Conditions, Further Possibilities of Development in Hungary). Budapest: Hungarian Central Statistical Office, 1990.

THE SMALL VENTURES AND OPENING TOWARD THE WORLD ECONOMY

Foreign trade was a state monopoly until 1987, and only the public foreign trade companies of the state could export and import. The long isolation from the foreign market kept the small entrepreneurs from utilizing foreign market opportunities despite their being opened for them in 1988. The direct export activity of the small entrepreneurs has been developing slowly.

At the same time, the entry of foreign capital is a remarkable development. Foreign capital—in addition to being used in the privatization of large companies and organizations—participated in the commercial prosperity of the small organizations as well. The number of joint ventures has been growing rapidly. At the end of 1988, their number was about 200, at the end of 1989 it was 900, and in late 1990 there are approximately 5,000. Their targets are the service sector. In about two-thirds of the joint ventures, the volume of the foreign capital investment has been under

Table 9.16
The Share of Small Ventures in the GDP by Organizational Form (in percentages)

Year	Small-scale Industry	Retail Trade	GMK (Economic Work Group)	PJT (Civil Incorporate Company)	VGMK (Corporate Economic Work Group)	ISZSZCS (Industrial and Service Cooperative Specialized Group)	Businesses Employing Less Than 100 Persons	Total
1981	3.8	0.3	--	--	--	--	0.7	4.8
1982	4.1	0.3	0.1	0.0	0.1	0.1	0.7	5.4
1983	4.7	0.5	0.4	0.0	0.7	0.4	1.5	8.2
1984	4.8	0.5	0.0	0.0	1.4	0.9	2.0	10.4
1985	5.1	0.6	1.1	0.0	1.7	1.1	2.0	11.6
1986	5.5	0.7	1.4	0.1	1.9	1.2	2.9	13.7
1987	5.6	0.8	1.4	0.1	1.6	1.0	4.1	14.6
1988	6.2	0.8	1.1	0.0	1.1	0.5	5.5	15.2

Source: Péter Pukli. A Kisvállakoz Helyzete, Működési Feltételei, További Fejlődési Lehetőségei Magyarországon (The Small Ventures: Place, Working Conditions, Further Possibilities of Development in Hungary). Budapest: Hungarian Central Statistical Office, 1990.

U.S.$15,000. Another fact also seems to prove that foreign capital investment in Hungary is oriented toward small ventures: 24 percent of the total small venture investment was realized in joint ventures. Nonetheless, the entry of foreign capital is not unobstructed. Difficulties derive from the lack of a business culture, bureaucratic restrictions, underdevelopment of the banking system, and the backwardness of the infrastructure.

EMPLOYMENT EFFECTS

In total, about 344,000 new jobs were created in the small-venture sector between 1981 and 1989. This is important because the number of employees nationally decreased slightly in this period.[9] The statement by Terez Laky (Karsai 1990), a well-known expert, that only small ventures have created new jobs, indicates the positive effect of the small ventures on employment. The importance of this effect can only grow. In October 1990, the official unemployment rate was only 1.4 percent and in November 1.6 percent, but all experts now expect a rapid growth of employment problems. The estimated projected unemployment rates range from 10 percent to as high as 20 percent of the work force.

The positive employment effect of the development of small ventures can be seen not only in their use of the redundant workers of the big firms. Their favorable influence on the structure of employment is equally important. People working in this dynamic sector—primarily the entrepreneurs themselves—are more educated, more qualified, have professional experiences from more places of work, and are more mobile, as seen in Tables 9.13 and 9.14.

From the point of view of employment, there is a paradox in the small-venture sector. This is the small entrepreneur who is a semi-entrepreneur, semi-state employee. Most small entrepreneurs are careful, judicious, and reflective. They usually do not plunge into the small venture. First, they try it as a second job, preserving their main employment in the public sector. According to the research of Terez Laky (Karsai 1990), the entrepreneurs typically prepare six to eight years for self-reliance, and they become solely entrepreneurs only when they are sure about their clients and market.

A portion of the entrepreneurs remain in the public sector even in the long run. They seek security in the public economy and luck in their "afternoon" private ventures. They maneuver in the gaps of these two types of economy. They often draw clients from the public enterprises to serve them in their private ventures. Many small entrepreneurs maintain their jobs in the public sphere in order to use the infrastructure (e.g., telephones, offices) of the public firm for private purposes. The entrepreneurs often make good use of the business relations established at the public enterprise. This issue is important because in analyzing the employment effects, the people in their main and supplementary employments must always be considered together.

NOTES

1. The present Hungarian statistical practice in listing small ventures includes private crafts workers, private retailers (small family ventures, in American terminology) as well as all economic organizations employing fewer than fifty persons.

2. Even in the agriculture cooperative, huge companies were established in the early 1970s, cooperatives such as the Egyesult Dunamenti Tsz. This cooperative engages in intensive farming, producing vegetables and fruits, and employing many thousands of people. It is 120 kilometers from one end to the other. Tractors and other machines made daily trips of thirty to fifty kilometers to cover the lands of the cooperative, hardly an efficient use of fuel.

3. In Hungary, trading activity is prohibited by law for economic work groups (GMK) and for VGM as well.

4. This is a special characteristic of the Hungarian economy. Such activities, mainly provided by exterior providers in the Western countries, resulted from the shortage of reliable contractors.

5. For more details about the fluctuation and bankruptcies of small ventures, see Gabor and Horvath (1987).

6. A sort of regulatory paradox is noticeable in this sector. While in the first half of the 1980s in particular, the state bureaucracy tried to fetter the small ventures by imposing thousands of petty rules on them, it could not sufficiently control the observance of these complicated rules. At the same time, some factors demanding certain regulations escaped the attention of the state. For example, there are 20,000 taxis in Budapest. The taxis work without almost any regulation and control. Anybody who has a driver's license can drive a taxi without taking into consideration the often terrible state of the car or the shocking ignorance of the driver.

This is not competition in the sense of a concerted and sane functioning of the economic cells, but rather chaos, a cancerous proliferation in the economy. In this connection, see the study of Berki (1990).

7. In addition to the success stories, the press furnishes many examples of fraudulent, swindling, Balkan-type variations on the new ventures.

8. The source of the data and tables published is Pukli (1990), pp. 93–97.

9. The number of active persons was 5 million in 1981, which decreased to 4.8 million in 1988. At the same time, the proportion of the employees of the small ventures increased from 2 percent in 1981 to 7.6 percent in 1988.

Chapter 10

Polish Firms in Transition

Mieczyslaw W. Socha and Urszula Sztanderska

During the first year of changing the Polish economy from a centrally planned to a market model, the most thorough changes have taken place in the area of macroeconomic policy. Transformation of the economic system in the state enterprise sector is considerably slower, holding back the pace of change in the entire national economy. The causes behind this sluggishness are the subject of this chapter.

We shall be seeking answers to the following three questions:

1. Did the enterprises have an awareness of the modalities involved in smooth adjustment to a market environment?
2. What constraints did they encounter in their actual efforts to adjust?
3. To what extent were they willing to abandon their traditional economic conduct under the impact of changed macroeconomic policies?

The main review will be preceded by a brief characterization of state enterprises prior to embarking on system changes, along with a presentation of their operations during the first eleven months of 1990.[1]

ENTERPRISE WITHOUT ENTREPRENEURSHIP

Polish enterprises at the close of 1989 differed substantially from the sort of companies functioning in the U.S. and West European economies. First, they operated in the non-private (state and cooperative) sector, which accounted for 80 percent of the gross domestic product and employed four-fifths of the national labor force. State enterprises were marked by a high concentration of production and a monopoly position on the domestic market. Out of some 6,000 state industrial enterprises (accounting for some 47 percent of the GDP), nearly 17 percent were large firms employing in excess of 1,000 people each and accounting for 65 percent of industrial output as well as nearly two-thirds of the total employment in industry.[2] Small firms, each employing fewer than 50 people, made up only 10 percent of the industrial landscape. Their share of output and employment was under 0.3 percent. No less than 70 percent of all industrial products were manufactured by firms enjoying monopoly positions in their fields.

The main form of organization was a self-managing enterprise with vaguely defined property rights, dispersed over numerous forms: state economic administrations (central and local) serving as so-called founding bodies (proxy owners) and finally the enterprise management. There are trade union locals in almost every enterprise, politically and organizationally split, and associated with either Solidarity or the OPZZ (All-Poland Alliance of Trade Unions, which came into being under martial law), or without any links to any of the national trade unions. At the end of 1989, the employers did not have their own organizations. Until its final collapse and formal dismantling, the Communist Party also had local cells in enterprises to—among other functions—exercise control over the filling of management posts. Such a multiplicity of decision-making authority in effect transferred the political struggle to the economy and was anything but conducive to efficient decision making.

The self-management bodies were conceived as something that could be designated a "collective employer." In practice, the self-management bodies acted more as quasi-trade unions, representing in particular the interests of employees. Some enterprises failed to organize self-management, and the tendency was to operate as a political foe of the authorities; employee councils were often used as a vehicle by Solidarity activists. Enterprise directors were formally subordinate to the self-management councils and the ministries (which had to accept the appointment of a director by the employee council and which also defined pay scales).

For the "founding bodies," an important objective was to preserve social peace in the enterprise. Hence, they lent little support to drives initiated by directors to improve the efficiency of operations, lest such a scheme contain the slightest threat of unemployment. Strike pressure was used by labor to force wage hikes and management changes or to put a stop to organizational change.

In theory, enterprises were autonomous. In practice, their decision-making autonomy was severely curtailed by state intervention. Enterprises could not make decisions by themselves about expansions, split-ups, mergers, liquidation, or price or wage policy. They also needed a state permit to carry out any foreign operations. Due to persistent shortages of production inputs, enterprises were forced to obtain the needed raw materials, feedstocks, foreign exchange, and to some extent, credits, through a system of central allocation.

Even though an enterprise was to finance its expenditures out of the revenues earned, if it ran short of funds, it could formally go bankrupt. In reality, it operated in an environment of "soft" financial constraints: soft-term loans (with interest rates lower than the rate of inflation), state budget subsidies, and various forms of tax relief. The taxation system was made up of a turnover tax as the prime form, taxes charged against costs (payroll and fixed assets), and taxes against profits. The aggregate tax for the state budget came to 80 to 90 percent of the profits generated.

In its operations, an enterprise encountered virtually no problems with demand, as in almost every field demand exceeded supply. Due to non-convertibility of the local currency, unrealistic exchange rates, state control over exports and imports, as well as the absence of foreign companies on the domestic market, the Polish enterprises operated in a closed economic environment.

Insufficient economic "stick" incentives (competition, the possibility of bankruptcy) and low rewards for good economic performance (profit was mostly skimmed off by the state budget, and salaries and bonuses for management were held down by administrative regulations) combined to suppress any interest in improving performance and taking economic risks.

Given the circumstances, the enterprises focused their efforts on a continuous contest with the central state economic administration to get a bigger share of the centrally allocated inputs, subsidies, credits, and a more preferential tax treatment.

Hyperinflation—there was a more than sixfold increase in the price level during 1989—linked with highly fluid rules of centrally set economic policies have contributed to shortening the horizon of decision making. Cost-benefit analyses of longer-term projects, particularly using marginal-type calculations, were almost unheard of.

SHOCK TREATMENT AND ENTERPRISE RESPONSE

Starting January 1, 1990, these enterprises found themselves in a radically different environment, forced by the orthodox plan to stabilize the economy and change it to a market model. First, there was a sweeping move away from state price controls (the share of freely shaped prices increased from 50 to 90 percent of all prices), while the officially set prices, where these continued to apply, were raised significantly. (This was particularly true of energy.) This was followed by the elimination of the central allocation of production inputs and foreign exchange.

Fiscal policy was reformed, changing from a deficit budget (11% of all budget spending) to a balanced budget by radically slashing subsidies (from 12 to 5% of GDP), raising the turnover tax rate (from 15 to 20%), raising the social security contribution (from 38 to 43%), eliminating tax relief, and reducing public sector spending.

A tight monetary policy was introduced along with a positive real interest rate (above the rate of inflation) and the elimination of concessional credits (with a few exceptions).

A policy of reining in enterprise spending on wages was pursued. The earlier full indexation was replaced with a 30 percent wage fund indexation for January, a 20 percent indexation for February through April, and a 60 percent indexation for May and June, along with a restrictive, punitive tax on any excess wage fund growth. (The marginal tax rate was 500% for each 1% by which the centrally set norm was exceeded.)

The *zloty* was devalued by setting a stable, yet freely floating exchange rate, coupled with domestic convertibility for current trade transactions. Rules governing exports and imports were greatly relaxed, and export surcharges were eliminated.

Anti-trust legislation was brought into play, and a policy was announced of privatizing the public sector, extending the banking and financial infrastructure, and in the coming years, replacing the turnover tax with a value-added tax, and the current tax on wage growth with a personal income tax.

Implementation of such sweeping economic decisions led to a new development for enterprises: the appearance of an aggregate demand barrier. Demand was down, due to reduced household sector buying (lower real income) and reduced buying by the government sector (reduced public sector spending). As a result, the structure of consumer demand and consumer behavior was altered.

In the initial stage, enterprises attempted to adjust to the new rules by reducing their business operations. After a preliminary build-up of inventory, the volume of production was cut, plants reduced work time by sending employees on forced leaves, some excess employment was trimmed, and attempts were made to redirect some of the output to export markets. In the first three months, industrial output declined 30 percent, employment was down 6 percent, and exports increased 2.7 percent. Even though the situation picked up a little in succeeding months, a sustained output growth did not prove possible. After the first eleven months of 1990, output was 25.4 percent lower than in the corresponding period of 1989, with employment in the five main sectors of the economy down 10.6 percent. A 10 percent increase in exports was insufficient to offset the decline in domestic demand.

Initially, the deepest fall in output was registered by the food processing and light industry sectors, and in the second quarter of 1990, the recession also hit the capital equipment and raw material-producing industries. After eleven months, industry continued to be most deeply affected by the recession, with a 38 percent decline in output.

The second reaction of enterprises was to significantly raise the prices for their wares. In January 1990, the prices for industrially manufactured goods rose 109.6 percent; in February they rose by another 9.6 percent, with the growth curve taking several months to level off. For enterprises, this marked a reaction to higher manufacturing costs (energy and bank credit costs were up, as was the cost of foreign exchange due to the devaluation of the *zloty*) and reflected their monopoly position in many markets. The price climb was particularly steep in areas in which earlier state price controls applied, in the fuels, energy and metallurgical sectors (more than a twelvefold growth in the first eleven months as compared with 1989). The slowest growth (less than sixfold) was registered in light industry, which had earlier sold its products at free market prices.

The industry response to tighter monetary policy was the nearly absolute withdrawal from taking bank credit in the first quarter, and retrenchment in investment activity. Investment outlays in the first eleven months were down nearly 12 percent as compared with the volume one year earlier.

Enterprises manifested considerable initial restraint in their wage policies, even falling below the limits allowed under wage policy guidelines. The consumer price index for January 1990 was up 78 percent, with pay in the five main sectors of the economy growing only 11 percent.

Moving into the second stage, enterprises mounted pressure on the government to loosen up the strings of economic policy, particularly in the area of credit, money, and wages. These pressures, exacerbated by a wave of strikes in late spring 1990, induced the government to ease the macroeconomic restrictions. These moves included a reduction in the interest rate, 100 percent wage indexation for July (reduced again to 60% in succeeding months), lower tax rates for exceeding the wage-growth ceilings, and reduced tariff rates. The government also stepped up its work on drafting privatization guidelines.

These moves allowed increases in household incomes and demand but brought little reaction in the form of higher supplies. Instead, the rate of inflation moved up once more. The prices for consumer goods and services, which in August 1990 rose no more than 1.8 percent, in succeeding months climbed at a rate of some 5 percent monthly. Output stabilized at a low level, and in October and November it declined about 1 percent, even though wages continued to climb at the rate of 10 percent in each of these months.

Recession also failed to speed up the rate of structural change, with the sole exception of exports. The reduced demand in the Council for Mutual Economic Assistance (CMEA) markets, with exports to that area declining 16 percent in the first eleven months, led to a change of focus for companies and increased exports to the West by more than 32 percent.

There was no transfer of idle fixed assets and labor to more productive uses. Not a single enterprise went bankrupt, and few new enterprises were formed in the state sector. There was a headlong increase in unemployment, from 50,000 in January to over one million by November (about 5.5% of the labor force), but the drop in employment was lower than the decline in production (for industry during the first eleven months, -8.9% and -25.4%, respectively).[3] Hence, the use of labor by enterprises became less efficient. No improvement was registered in paying for real effort exerted by labor, with the highest wages continuing to go to employees of the largest, though not necessarily the most efficient, plants.

The adjustment in technology has been imperceptible. No new technologies or new products have come on stream, and little attention is being paid to the quality aspect of production.

MARKET ECONOMY: UNEXPLORED TERRITORY FOR POST-COMMUNIST ENTERPRISES

Polish state enterprises have neither the theoretical background nor the practical skills needed for effective operation in a market environment.[4]

It is estimated that between 50 and 80 percent of top management people in enterprises are totally unsuitable for their posts, despite formally high qualifications. There are several explanations for this:

1. Schooling in the area of management and economy was geared to the requirements of a centrally planned economy, and the knowledge imparted on the functioning of the market was only surface-deep and often distorted.

2. A high proportion of managers have no formal training at all in management or economics. Most Polish directors have engineering degrees, according to the role of enterprises as mainly executors of production.

3. The advancement criteria for enterprise managers were, and continue to be, under a heavy shadow of political consideration. Earlier, it was important whether someone was a holder of the Communist Party card or toed the party line; currently, the very same traits have become a disqualifying factor, irrespective of actual management skills.

4. State enterprises have failed to develop a mechanism for selecting managers according to some tangible criteria that would allow for career planning and for defining the responsibilities for company performance. In effect, management posts in the state sector are relatively unattractive, leading the best potential people to seek their material and professional rewards in other areas.

5. Most of the management people never had any direct contact with the market in their careers. The state monopoly on foreign trade is carried out by a very few monopoly trade offices, and it is only the staff of those offices that has earned some practical skills in operating in an international market environment.

A still lower level of skill is represented by the employee self-management councils, which in state enterprises have a sweeping range of decision-making rights. Trade union leaders also have limited knowledge of the impact markets exert on enterprise standing, and the interrelation between this and the situation of employees.

The main areas in which Polish managers lack skills include: financial management issues, including bookkeeping, which could serve as a useful management information tool; conducting negotiations within the enterprise; and arranging efficient organizational structures. Managers also suffer from catastrophic illiteracy in foreign languages. While preparations for the introduction of Western accounting standards and training for the accounting staffs are well under way, bridging the information gap in the remaining areas may prove extremely difficult. Enterprises have problems with such elementary issues as the use of promissory notes and such fundamental questions as mapping out a strategy for capital formation. These are completely unknown issues for Polish managers. Considering that the capital market is only beginning to take shape in the country, the managers cannot gain experience from developed, stable market mechanisms. Setting up management studies that correspond to Western business administration curricula is now only at the discussion stage. It is estimated that Poland has no more than between twenty and fifty professors with the qualifications to offer management training.[5]

Most enterprises are helpless when faced with diminishing returns. They have proven themselves incapable of identifying the required directions of restructuring. Assistance has been proffered by Western consulting companies for the first and very best enterprises due for privatization. Domestic consulting companies are still few and far between, and even these lack the experience to identify ways for overcoming the economic quagmire of large enterprises.

Western experts also point to many areas completely unknown to Polish managers, in which the managers do not realize their lack of knowledge. These include market segmentation and marketing,[6] the art of a planned conduct for business, the capacity to get all parts of the enterprise working toward higher added value, the ways of attaining higher product quality and higher productivity, personnel policy issues, acquaintance with European and global markets and their inherent legal and social aspects, and the ways of collecting, storing and processing data concerning the enterprise and its working environment.

INTERNAL AND EXTERNAL CONSTRAINTS ON EFFICIENT DECISION MAKING

Even enterprises with an efficient managing staff will face numerous constraints preventing them from operating in a manner similar to that of Western companies.

The first group of constraints stems from a dispersion of property rights in enterprises and the specific, powerful position of employees, with the relatively weaker position of management. In enterprises, the rule- and decision-making authority is split between the employee council (elected by all employees) and the director.[7] In certain cases, some of these rights accrue also to the state administration representing the State Treasury. Reforms instituted in 1990 have deprived the administration of the right to intervene directly in enterprise affairs, giving the enterprises a much wider autonomy. Yet this has led to a situation in which an enterprise faces no pressures from owners expecting profits. State Treasury expectations in this respect have been replaced by a 20 percent tax on enterprise assets (a "dividend" tax).

The employees, in turn, appear solely to seek the maximum pay, and the only restraining factor here seems to be the steeply graduated tax on increasing the payroll above the normative indexing coefficient. The director, appointed jointly by the employees and state administration, is to a large extent subordinated to the employees; in the case of their dissatisfaction, he could be fired from his post. The state administration, needing industrial calm, will lend no support to the director in such a case.[8] One notes enterprise payroll padding up to the limits of the steep tax, regardless of economic performance. Enterprises that have scored major strides in profits, mainly due to their skill in adjusting to the curbs in demand on the domestic market or thanks to successful entry into foreign markets, still cannot attract more or better skilled labor to their enterprises, as wage growth is limited by the tax system. In turn, enterprises with low and falling profits continued to pay high wages, again up to the tax limit, even at the cost of reducing profits.

Employee pressures also extend to maintaining full employment, regardless of production requirements. Surveys indicate that employment dropped in much the same proportion for most industrial enterprises, even though some of these were dynamically expanding their output and others were reducing output (and profits as well). Hence, for most enterprises the cost element lacks flexibility and is similar in nature to fixed costs.

Note should also be taken of the inflexibility of labor within enterprises and labor resistance to changing the scope of responsibilities, working hours, more intensive work, and retraining in new skills. The force of this resistance has weakened somewhat in recent months, as unemployment has increased.

Trade unions are also placed differently in Poland, as compared with Western countries. Two, sometimes even three different and competing trade unions within a single enterprise often step outside the bounds of protecting employee rights. They often manifest ambitions of co-managing the plant, frequently embracing political causes and thereby creating a highly unstable balance of interests within an enterprise.

The second group of constraints stemming from within are the legal regulations preventing full liquidity of the enterprise cash flow (the mandatory enterprise funds), the complex and highly redistributive tax system, and the rules limiting the freedom to shape employee pay as needed. These constraints are a legacy of the past. Nonetheless, their early elimination is not possible, as long as property rights are not defined clearly and the director is not given some real power to manage. These constraints are viewed as "props" built into the system of an ailing enterprise, serving to dampen wage demands and safeguard development of the enterprise itself. As with most props, these have their drawbacks, as they do not allow an enterprise to freely use the available cash resources and lead to the danger of their inefficient allocation.[9]

The third group of constraints is set by the shortage of development funds. Enterprises as a rule are undercapitalized for investment purposes, and between 20 and 30 percent of their working capital is in the form of credit. Chances are dim for increasing equity, given the restrictive monetary policy and very modest resources held by households. The 1990 price increases have eroded the value of household savings, and the drop in real incomes caused redirection of a part of these savings for the maintenance of buying power. The continuing relatively high inflation makes investment decisions risky, especially considering that the interest rate has remained high and fluctuated widely. (Until July 1990, it was defined as a "per month" rate; currently it is defined as a yearly rate, but continues to be unstable.) The inaugurated privatization was to yield additional equity for enterprises, but the two objectives, privatization plus injection of capital, are difficult to reconcile. Given that the book value of the assets of state enterprises is worth some eight times more than the entire financial reserves of the population, and considering the intent to privatize quickly, the shortage of freely available capital funds seems obvious.[10] Continuing restrictive monetary and fiscal policy, made necessary due to inflation, wrecks the chance of stimulating domestic demand. Enterprises have proved incapable of reducing costs during the first year of reforms, and there is little ground to believe that such reductions will materialize in succeeding years. Given this, one cannot expect a capacity from within the enterprises to quickly increase profits and thus the availability of funds for development.

There could be expectations, however, of more differentiation in the material standing of enterprises and, on this basis, of funds finding their way to the most efficient enterprises. This development is checked by the surfacing of involuntary interenterprise crediting, by the expedient of customers failing to pay for their supplies on time. Such unpaid claims represent around 50 percent of the value of monthly sales. This reflects negatively on enterprise results, since the enterprises become providers of free credit. This interenterprise crediting acts as a brake on the reallocation of inefficiently deployed productive resources.

Fourth, monopolization of the economy, Polish-style, is similar to the existence of mammoth enterprises with close vertical integration and with very limited autonomy for the various segments of such enterprises, making them inflexible in adapting to changes in the external environment. Economic results for the first six months of 1990 confirmed the claim that the giant enterprises fared worse than average.[11] Restructuring them will take money and time.

External constraints on the market-oriented adjustment of enterprises stem from the less than complete abandonment of an administrative approach to macroeconomic policy. Up to the end of 1990, there was still only the barest outline of a capital market and its usual institutions.

There is no flexible labor market; the main barrier to this is the shortage of housing and the legally petrified structure of house ownership and occupancy. Restructuring of the banking system is proceeding with great difficulty, and the procedures to be followed in applying for credit still smack of old administrative ways, with economic criteria only secondary. Parameters of the economic decisions that have to be taken into account by enterprises are in a state on constant flux (customs tariff, interest rate, etc.). Many legal regulations of fundamental importance to enterprises are only in the very early stages of the legislative process, such as the labor code and changes in the fiscal system. The market infrastructure (e.g., insurance, banking, securities market, telecommunications) is still all but non-existent. This, along with many of the institutions that make up the operating environment for enterprises, prevents Polish enterprises from behaving in the same way as companies in developed market economies.

The situation of Polish enterprises was further exacerbated by unforeseen developments: the price shock due to higher oil prices in the aftermath of the Gulf crisis, a 40 percent reduction in supplies from the Soviet Union (with crude oil figuring prominently on this list), and a collapse in demand for Polish products from the traditional top two markets, the Soviet Union and East Germany.

INCENTIVES AND DISINCENTIVES IN ADAPTING TO DEMAND

Enterprise behavior includes elements of reaction typical of new macroeconomic environments, some of which are unique to Poland, both at times of a sharp rollback in demand and when demand increases, as in mid-1990.

Enterprises did not make full use of the opportunity to improve the efficiency of their own operations and change their market position by seeking out more attractive offers of input supplies and markets for their products. It is generally believed that the cause here, next to the lack of skills and the limited possibilities, was the lack of motivation for reoriented enterprise operations.

First, the profitability of enterprises in 1989 and in early 1990 improved, thanks to the possibility of raising the prices of wares produced with materials purchased at earlier, much lower prices. Because of this, the imperative to restructure enterprises lost much of its teeth. It was only during the second quarter that the financial consequences of reduced demand began to be felt by some enterprises in the form of lower sales and profitability. The earlier strategy of continuing production at un-changed levels and building up stocks of unsold products was replaced with a strategy of cutting back production and reducing orders for raw materials. This was not true in every enterprise, and the steel industry could be a case in point.

Adaptation on the side of outlays was fairly standard. Enterprises that dynamically increased sales and those that faced a collapse of their markets have made very modest cuts in employment. Those that increased pay up to the threshold at which the special tax comes into play achieved modest reductions in material production costs (with the exception of the food processing industry, which profited from a relative reduction in the cost of farm produce as compared with the preceding year).

One could also note some shift in the product mix to cheaper grades of consumer products, as firms adjusted to a less well-off customer. Yet one could hardly speak of real incentives to improve quality or to reduce the average cost and prices of the old product range.

The weakness of market incentives was due primarily to the weak nature of rewards to be reaped by an enterprise daring to pursue a more ambitious adjustment program.

The salaries of directors were largely unconnected with the financial performance of their enterprises. Such a link was not established until 1990, and then only for some directors. At the same time, directors were banned from owning shares in companies set up by the enterprises that they manage. This ban was due to suspicions of dishonesty in pricing the physical assets contributed as company equity, but the side effect was to create disincentives. One should keep in mind that the "old" managers had to operate in an environment of a bitter political campaign launched around mid-year against the directors, who had earlier belonged to or collaborated with the Communist Party.

Seeing the process of pauperizing the society and the decline in real wages, enterprise employees, drawing on their earlier experience, treated any increases in pay as no more than compensation for the higher price levels, and expected their management to use all necessary funds available for this purpose.[12] No mental link was established between pay hikes and the need to make some more thorough changes within the enterprises. The wage hikes were small, as set against the increases in living costs and against the general increase in aggregate household income, which was padded by welfare benefits and incomes earned in the private sector, including the "underground," or unregistered, economy. In view of this, pay increases in state enterprises lost their incentive role. Due to these reasons, and to a very egalitarian philosophy to which most employees subscribed, pay scales within enterprises continued to be fairly standard and non-differentiated, further eroding the motivational role of wages. Employee pressures on management also extend to questions of guaranteed employment; hence, employment was reduced on a limited scale and was largely unrelated to changes in production rates.

In enterprises in which employee self-management councils played a more active role, their focus was set on guaranteeing employee forms of ownership, modeled on the U.S. experience with ESOPs (Employee Stock Ownership Plans).

Both the employee councils and the trade unions as a rule spoke out against the influx of foreign capital, believing that this would undermine their standing. For the same reason, they frequently spoke out against privatizing, even commercializing enterprises, fearing a stronger role of management.

Given the circumstances, most enterprises adopted a wait-and-see attitude. A unique balance of interests was struck between the leading interest groups in enterprises, with little done in the area of organizational change. The directors did not fire workers and did not exact labor discipline more strictly than before; workers refrained from protest actions; the employee councils made no attempt to dismiss the director. This was helped by the fact that even large-scale cost-cutting made little dent in the economic standing of the enterprise. Wages, on average, account for some 10 percent of costs and even less in some industries (in metallurgy, 3.5%; in food processing, 7%).

Another factor weakening the motivation to restructure enterprises was the mounting struggle within the Solidarity camp, followed by a presidential campaign in which populist slogans disclaimed any need for such major hardships and deprivation just for the sake of system changes. Promises were made to switch to new macroeconomic policies, and wage demands were thus pressed with force. The big-industry workers asked to be rewarded for their contribution to toppling the communist system. For instance, workers of the Gdansk shipyard demanded the company assets, free of charge (a bill to this effect was tabled within the parliament). Within Solidarity structures, the employees of big enterprises set up a substructure, called Network, to act as a political pressure group for employee stock ownership and the elimination of the tax on payroll increases. The top enterprises that actively championed softer government policies were the giant establishments that function in something less than a true free-market style: the railways, public utility companies and coal mines.

Pressing claims on outside parties, instead of competing aggressively on the market and restructuring firms, is simply easier when that bankruptcy is only a theoretical threat. The recovery procedures instituted in enterprises qualifying for bankruptcy entailed no true hardships for the employees.

WHERE DO WE GO FROM HERE?

It becomes clear from this chapter that the orderly arrangement of ownership issues and industrial relations in the state sector is a fundamental precondition for speeding up both the enterprise transformation and an effective adaptation to the emergent market situation. Privatization would seem the most desirable solution here. The private economy, far from going into recession, has achieved a 9 percent growth in output. Nevertheless, further success requires time and foreign equity investment.

Accepting that the form of state enterprises will be with us for some time to come, especially in the primary materials and heavy industry sectors, there is a need to revamp the system of property rights, and in particular bolster the position of management in the running of enterprises. This entails considerable shrinking or even elimination of the decision-making rights currently accruing to self-management councils. The present formula of trade union rights in enterprises cannot be reconciled with the requirement to speedily transform the system. Trade unions will either have to limit themselves to their classic role as watchdog over labor relations and wages or accept greater responsibility for the consequences of their actions.

A fundamental problem is the manner of countering employee pressures for higher wages when enterprises switch over to new functioning modes. Foundations have to be built into the system for solid public conviction that the only way to increase real earnings and to reduce the number of jobless is to improve productivity and profits. Overcoming workers' reluctance to change is possible if enterprises are given a free hand in setting their wages. But giving enterprises such freedom without first addressing the questions of ownership and industrial relations could result in inflation.

Success in the changes carried out is heavily contingent on the continuation of policies that apply economic force to bring about enterprise reorganization. Easing the strings just to obtain some short-run political gains could put off enterprise restructuring and thereby increase the social costs of the operation in the future.

NOTES

1. Unless otherwise noted, all statistics are from data of the Central Statistical Office (1990). Unless otherwise stated, the change indices compare the first eleven months of 1990 with the first eleven months of 1989.

2. In contrast to the public sector, the private business sector, apart from agriculture, as of December 1989 was made up of 860,000 firms employing approximately 1,780,000 people, meaning that average employment was two people per firm. The vast majority of private firms are no more than craft workshops using little hired labor.

3. A good part of the present unemployment is voluntary, the result of liberal unemployment benefits. The numbers of unemployed also consist of people who have never held a job and who are not looking for work. So-called group layoffs account for no more than 11 percent of unemployment.

4. A similar situation prevails in private enterprises.

5. A few private schools have been established in this field, effectively offering retraining courses. Their curricula are thought to place too much emphasis on theory.

6. In early 1990, nearly all enterprises continued producing at a rate unchanged from the close of 1989, even though they could have expected reduced demand. It was only the ninefold increase in inventories of unsold products that forced enterprises to reduce output. The first phase of recession affected the consumer goods industries and could have been expected to extend to the manufacturers of industrial supply products. (In steel there was an eightfold build-up of unsold inventories.)

7. The decision-making powers of employee self-management include defining changes in the direction of enterprise operations; acceptance of the balance sheet; investment decisions; endorsement of decisions to sell off fixed assets, split up the enterprise, or enter into joint ventures with other enterprises; and deciding the distribution of profits.

8. Strikes to bring about the dismissal of management were not unusual.

9. In the private sector, there are no such constraints on the liquidity of company funds, but the tax system extends to all sectors.

10. According to government estimates disclosed in the address to parliament delivered by Finance Deputy Minister W. Misiag on December 13, 1990.

11. Starting in the second quarter of 1990, an inverse relation was registered between the change in sales and size of enterprise, indicating that small firms adapted better to changes in demand.

12. This becomes understandable when one considers that the average real wage in the state sector in 1989 was at the 1978 level, and during the first ten months of 1990 it went down approximately 17 percent.

Chapter 11

The Role of Peasants in the Systemic Transformation of the Polish Economy, 1944–1990

Jerzy Wilkin

The history of peasants and of the peasant economy in socialist countries is one of the stormiest, most dramatic and most complex elements of recent history. This history, despite the differences and deviations in particular socialist countries, to a substantial degree has modified the shape of the economies and the societies—their social institutions, fundamental rights, and legal regulations.

The continuation of the peasant (or quasi-peasant) economy in all socialist countries, the persistent fight of the peasants for survival, and the weaknesses of the collective forms of management and organization in agriculture have resulted in demands from the peasants for qualitatively greater changes in the socialist economic system than were called for by any other major social group.

The establishment of the new political and economic order in Poland after World War II did not result in an elimination of peasantry and the peasant economy. On the contrary, it brought the petrification of the peasant nature of Polish agriculture and arrested the process of transformation of peasants into farmers. In the beginning of the 1990s, no more than one out of ten private farms in Poland could be termed as farmer type. In this regard, Poland remains a curious phenomenon among the European countries.

The rural population constitutes a very large portion of the total population in Poland, as indicated in Table 11.1. Peasants operating private farms constitute the majority of the rural population. This is also reflected in the structure of farmland used by different sectors (private, state, and cooperative), as shown in Table 11.2.

Table 11.1
Population of Poland, 1946–1988 (in thousands)

Years	Total	Rural	Rural as % of Total
1946	23,640	15,597	66.0
1950	25,035	15,792	63.0
1960	29,795	15,394	51.7
1970	32,658	15,570	47.7
1980	35,735	14,756	41.3
1988	37,775	14,648	38.8

Source: Rocznik Statystyczny (Statistical Yearbook). Warsaw: Głowny Urzad Statystyczny (Polish Central Statistics Office), various years.

Table 11.2
Structure of Farmland Use in Selected Years (in percentages)

Year	Private	State	Cooperative
1946	93.2	6.8	–
1950	89.3	9.9	0.8
1960	86.9	11.9	1.2
1970	83.5	14.8	1.7
1980	74.5	20.0	5.5
1988	76.4	19.8	3.8

Source: Rocznik Statystyczny (Statistical Yearbook). Warsaw: Główny Urząd Statystyczny (Polish Central Statistics Office), various years.

PEASANTS AND AGRICULTURAL POLICY IN A SOCIALIST STATE: THE STRUGGLE FOR SURVIVAL

The year 1944 opened a new stage of agricultural policy in Poland. Since the beginning of the socialist state, there has been distrust toward it among the peasant farmers. This was the result, first of all, of the fear of collectivization, the effects of which, with the example of the Soviet Union, were known to many peasants before World War II. The distrust of peasants toward the new socialist authorities affected their attitude to the agrarian reform being implemented. Despite the universal longing for farmland, the break-up of the large estates did not meet with universal enthusiasm from the farmers. The attitude toward the agrarian reform was most positive in the most overpopulated and poorest farming regions (such as the Rzeszów, Kielce, or Kraków regions in south Poland). Much less positive was the attitude toward parcelization of estates as observed in the Poznań and Pomorze regions. The demand for farmland was smaller there, the standard of living of farm workers in those estates was better (at times superior to that of owners of small farms elsewhere), but, more importantly, large modern farms were highly regarded in those regions. A sizeable number of those who agreed to accept the parcelled farmland returned it after a few months. As Slabek writes (1978), in the second half of 1945, such returns in some regions exceeded 80 percent.

As the following years have shown, agrarian reform in post-World War II Poland was only a short-term tactical action that was meant to attract the peasant masses to the socialist state and its system of authority. The distrust of farmers toward the new authorities proved to be justified. In 1947, after the meeting of nine communist and worker parties in Szklarska Poreba in Poland, the movement toward collectivization of the countryside began. The collectivization resulted in anti-state attitudes among the peasants and, contrary to its original intentions, consolidated the countryside and strengthened the attachment to the land. In many cases, the collectivization was appalling, as was the agricultural policy pursued.

Collectivization was accompanied in Poland by an economic drain of the countryside. The obligatory deliveries (administratively decreed sales of products by farmers) at prices below actual production costs were expanded. The private farming sector was clearly discriminated against during the Six-Year Plan (1950–1955) in the allocation of production inputs. As much as two-thirds of the investment outlays were earmarked for the state and cooperative farm sectors.

Bleak development perspectives and a shrinking in financial potential resulted, for the majority of peasant farms, in a slowing down of the investment, and in many cases in actual decapitalization of fixed production assets. The farmers reacted to collectivization with a defeatist attitude. In the years 1951 and 1952, total agricultural production declined, and in the six-year period between 1950 and 1955, farm output per capita in Poland failed to increase. This was, in fact, a defeat for the agricultural policy implemented by the state.

The departure from the policy of forced collectivization after 1956 was in turn a great victory for the Polish peasants. Private farmers reacted quickly and positively to the improvement in economic conditions of the private farming sector. A tangible growth of agricultural production and an improvement in market supply had, no doubt, a stabilizing impact on the social situation during the first years of the Wladyslaw Gomulka regime. However, in the 1960s, the positive incentives set into motion after October 1956 gradually disappeared, and by the end of the decade, the situation in many parts of the agricultural sector was close to stagnation. There was no concept of developing the private farm sector; growth of bigger private farms was arrested, and prospects for the further socialist transformations of Polish agriculture did not favor the development of the majority of farms. The critical situation in agriculture was without doubt one of the factors that led to the December 1970 events and the displacement of a part of the ruling regime.

The beginning of the 1970s brought further favorable changes in the conditions in which private farms operated. As the most important changes in this respect one may recognize the departure from the system of obligatory deliveries (sales) of farm products and the inclusion of private farmers into the national health care system. Profitability of farm production was improved, and supplies of inputs for farmers increased. The years 1971 to 1973 were a period of unusually rapid growth of farm production, in particular of livestock production. The number of swine was 62 percent higher in 1974 than in 1970. The final three years of the 1970s brought growth, on the average, at a rate of more than 7 percent per annum. Such high figures of production growth in agriculture are very rarely to be found, not only in Poland, but throughout the world.

The year 1974 saw still another change in agricultural policy, this time clearly against the private farm sector. This was apparent particularly in the distribution of production inputs (investment goods, mineral fertilizers, etc.), in the transfer of farmland from the State Land Fund (sales of farmland to private farmers were almost stopped), and in the allocation of credits and subsidies. The policies were yet another effort to accelerate the "socialization" of agriculture, that is, to strengthen the position of the state and cooperative farms in the structure of Polish agriculture. One must add that this was a failed effort, as were the previous ones. However, the costs of this last attempt were exceedingly high and, to a large extent, contributed to the social and economic crisis at the end of the 1970s and beginning of the 1980s. Once again, the awakened hopes and expectations of peasants for a permanent improvement of development prospects for their farms were dashed.

During the post-World War II period, one may note three development cycles in agriculture that were initiated by important changes in the state agricultural policy. Crises appeared in agriculture in the first half of the 1950s, at the end of the 1960s, and in the second half of the 1970s. In each case, the most important source of the crisis was a movement to limit the development of private farms.

These attempts were, to a large extent, abandoned by the authorities in view of the slow-down or decline of agricultural production and the social repercussions of the agricultural crisis. After each of the crises, farmers gained advantages in the spheres of the institutional, legal, social, and economic systems. After 1980, relatively important changes took place in the conditions of the private farming sector as a result of the acute crisis during the four decades of the postwar period. As the most important change, one may name the constitutional guarantee of the permanence of private farms. After each crisis, agriculture was an important element stabilizing the national economic and social situation. It was found that private farmers would react very quickly to the improved economic conditions, in particular to improved profitability of farm production. The propensity for capital accumulation is high in most peasant farms, which means that farmers react to a significant growth of incomes with a higher increase of accumulation than of consumption. In general, one may assess that the response of peasant farms to economic incentives is high, but that this phenomenon has not been properly utilized in agricultural policy.

The strong links of a large part of Polish society with land and farming, in view of fluctuations in agricultural policy and significant insecurity as concerns the future of private farms, have resulted in a growth of the number of farms run by part-time farmers who hold other jobs outside the farm. This category may include about 65 percent of peasant farms. The dual sources of income are viewed by farmers as a double security for their welfare. Pluri-active farms proved to be unusually durable and the number of these farms is rising continuously. The mass character of pluri-activity has contributed to the fragmentation of Polish agriculture which, in comparison with other European countries, is most anachronistic in this respect. This is, however, the result of the generally faulty agricultural policy, which was trying to reconcile long-term ideological goals with the exigencies of the economic situation.

ADJUSTMENT MECHANISM OF THE PEASANT ECONOMY TO THE CENTRALLY PLANNED ECONOMIC SYSTEM

Why did peasants as a social class and producer-type survive in the socialist system? This question is of particular importance in Poland. I am not capable of answering this question in full. I would like to indicate, however, some circumstances that have favored the conservation of the peasant system in the socialist state. The first was the strong resistance of peasants to their transformation into a group of collective farm producers. This resistance had substantial support among the inhabitants of towns. One should not disregard the differences in views on this matter among the representatives of the authorities, which led to hesitation in the actual realization of the socialist transformation in Polish agriculture.

The other factor, which probably was of decisive importance for maintaining or, more exactly, tolerating the existence of the peasant sector, was the low effectiveness of the socialized sector of agriculture. Polish sociologist Krzysztof Gorlach called this type of governmental policy toward peasant agriculture, which was implemented in the 1960s and 1970s, "a repressive tolerance" (Gorlach 1989). Until recently, the representatives of the central political authorities in Poland did not hide their belief that the socialization of agriculture was but a question of time. The issue that would decide the speed of this process was the technical possibility of substituting production produced by the private sector with production from the socialized sector, possibly supplemented by imports from abroad. The factor correcting this rate of socialist transformation of agriculture was the state of national feeling and public reactions, the latter being determined by the level of market supply of food products. The importance of these conditions and circumstances is witnessed by the fact that whenever the production results of agriculture (the supply of food and farm products) relatively improved, the offensive would be started in favor of expanding the socialist sector and constraining the private one. This process would in turn be arrested in periods of deterioration of production and the resulting stresses. Thus, it was not the power and might of the peasant economy but the weakness of the socialized sector of the economy that was the principal reason for the survival of such a large private sector in Poland.

Similar conditions have appeared, although on a different scale in the other socialist countries. In Yugoslavia, despite the clear preferences for the socialized farms, it was not possible to alter the structure of agriculture during the last three decades. In countries where agriculture has been collectivized, it proved necessary to maintain rather substantial enclaves of subsidiary farms as an economic buffer. This proved to be of particular importance in periods of difficulty in the development of socialist agriculture. Even in Hungary, a country with a relatively well-functioning socialized agricultural sector, the production success of agriculture was achieved through the skillful utilization of both the collective forms of work organization and of individual-work or family-work farms. In an interesting and extensive empirical monograph on Hungarian agriculture, Nigel Swine has demonstrated that for efficient and productive operation, it proved necessary to combine what he terms "family labor" with "socialist wage labor." Thus, large-scale collective production and small-scale commodity production were based on individual (family) labor. This generalization extends as well to the other socialist countries (Swine 1985).

The most spectacular example of a failed effort to outlaw the peasant economy and to replace it with fully collectivized farming is the People's Republic of China. A tragic experiment was the agrarian communism of Pol Pot in Cambodia.

Returning to the case of Polish agriculture, I would like to refer to the concepts of autonomous functions and the functions of higher-level and primary adjustment in economic systems, as explained by Janos Kornai (Kornai 1971). The experience of Polish agriculture in the past four decades demonstrates the enormous potential and efficiency of the autonomous functions of the peasant economy. This observation is supported by the experience of many centuries in numerous countries. Particularly efficient proved to be the autonomous functions and the primary adjustment demonstrated by the peasant farms in periods of crisis.

The most recent example is found in the reactions of peasants in Poland to the economic crisis, which started at the end of the 1970s and early 1980s. I have no doubt that the efficiency of the autonomous functions on the average peasant farm is much greater than in the average socialized enterprise. The socialist units of the economy, devoid of many rather basic decision prerogatives and accustomed to a higher degree of paternalism from the state, have developed negligible adjustment potential and, in more difficult economic conditions, have had problems with normal functioning. The new developments in East European countries in 1989 and in 1990 have further validated my opinions.

The peasant farms were among those few economic entities in which the unity of work, management, and ownership was maintained. This permitted direct linkage of management functions, executive action, division of incomes, and decisions concerning development and their placement in the same hands. Such a situation created chances for rapid and efficient adjustment reactions and for a favorable incentive climate. This last aspect is of particular importance for the survival of the peasant economy in socialism. There is a rather universal view, which I share, that the motivational system in the peasant economy is the principal source of its strength, while the insufficiencies of the incentive system in the socialized economy are its weakness.

While the sphere of current activities of peasant farms and what we have termed "primary adjustment" were controlled for the major part by the peasant themselves, the development processes of this economy remained under the control of the dominating socialist system. The instruments of this control were of a legal, administrative, and economic nature. The state authorities rather effectively constrained area expansion and the production growth of the peasant farms through farmland transfer and taxation policies. In addition, the state controlled the flow of industrial inputs to the peasant farms and acted as a monopoly in the procurement of many farm staples. Thus, we may say that the secondary adjustment, which was linked with development and modernization, was fundamentally controlled by the political and economic center of the country. The policy of obligatory deliveries by the peasant farms to the state procurement system at government-fixed, depressed prices was economically irrational.

To sum up, we may say that the primary adjustment of peasant farms to the system of the socialist economy in Poland proved to be fully effective. The very significant quality differences in the characteristics of the subsystem of the peasant economy and of the dominating system of the socialist system proved, however, to be an obstacle to the broader development and modernization of the peasant economy. The systemic alienation of the peasant economy was acutely experienced both in the ideological and in the political spheres, as well in strictly economic terms. As a result, the secondary adjustment of the peasant economy was made difficult and constrained and remained under the careful control of the center.

In the decades of existence of the socialist economic system, gradual but significant changes were taking place within the system itself. Among the most important of these we may name: a gradual growth of the importance of market mechanisms; a partial decentralization of economic decisions, including decisions on the development and allocation of resources; a reduction in the discriminatory treatment of the private sector; and a growing importance of economic calculations as a basis for decisions. In the case of Poland, these changes were enforced to a major degree by the existence of a large sector of the peasant economy. This may sound paradoxical, but the peasants proved to be a social group that forced progress toward rationality in economic management (Wilkin 1986). The differences that today distinguish the peasant economy from the dominating post-socialist economy are no longer as great as they were in the 1950s and the 1960s. It was not Polish socialism that "tamed" the peasant economy and peasants; rather, the peasants transformed socialism. The homogenization of the system was slow but clearly visible. It was accompanied by the influence exerted by peasants on many other spheres of social and cultural life. Jan Szczepański has shown in his research the phenomena of "ruralization of urban culture" and "peasantification of the worker class" (Szczepański 1975).

THE GREAT SYSTEM TRANSFORMATION AND PEASANT FARMING: FIRST EXPERIENCE

The political changes that have recently taken place in a number of socialist countries in Central and Eastern Europe initiated the principal changes in the economic systems of these countries. The purpose of these changes was the creation of a market economy, similar to those in the developed capitalist countries. Among the socialist countries, the most advanced in this process is Poland. Replacement of the administratively allocated economy by a market one started first in the sector of private agriculture and the food economy. As of January 1, 1990, these principles of economies and management also included the other sectors of the national economy.

The change from a centrally planned, command economy to a market economy linked to a fundamental change of the political and state institutions deserves the name of the "great system transformation," as has been used in regard to the transfer from the feudal formation to capitalism. The process differs, however, in two important ways. The transformation of the system in countries of Central and Eastern Europe is taking place on a different, and higher, level of development than the transfer from feudalism to capitalism, and this change is also taking place at a much more rapid pace than before, although it is difficult at present to say when it will end.

Because private family farms dominate Polish agriculture, the principles of market operations were in force over the past decades for this sector much more than for the other sectors. Nevertheless, the experiences of Polish peasants during the introduction of market mechanisms are not positive. The liberalization from state control of farm product prices, as well as those of farming inputs necessary for agricultural production, proved to be a far from favorable development for most farmers. The dictatorship of the administrative state system was replaced by a dictatorship of monopolies in farm products procurement, as well as in processing and trade of farm products. Despite the many-fold growth of prices of food products in Poland in a space of several months, the profitability of farm production actually went down. In addition to the monopolistic practices of the institutions cooperating with agriculture, another factor contributing to the deterioration of the economic situation of farmers was the decline of real incomes of the population and the ensuing drop in demand for food. For the first time in some decades, Poland witnessed a surplus of farm products and storage problems. This occurred despite the generally high rate of inflation in the national economy in a period of three months, and in the face of rather substantial decreases in the price of meat, butter, and sugar.

In contrast to the highly developed capitalist countries, where state intervention in agriculture is aimed at easing the unfavorable conditions for overproduction, in the socialist countries the efforts of the state were aimed instead in the direction of stimulating the growth of farm output. The situation has changed, at least in Poland and in Hungary. Farmers in Poland are beginning to insist on a more active role of the state in order to improve their income and profitability of farm production. One of the agents of this change is to be the Agricultural Market Agency. Farmers have also demanded that the government allocate preferential credits for agriculture, determine minimum guaranteed prices for farm products, as well as allocate subsidies to some products sold by farmers. The majority of these demands have been rejected by the government. The economic policy of the current government is dominated by the neo-liberal philosophy and its priorities are reducing inflation, eliminating the state budget deficit, replacing the planned economy with a market system, and restructuring the national economy. These overall principles do not agree with propositions that seek to allocate special privileges or preferences to one or another part of the economy. The targets and principles of the economic policy implemented by the Polish government in 1989 are accepted by the majority of the public, despite the clearly apparent recessionary effects of this policy during 1990.

In the beginning of 1989, when intensive discussions were held on the future shape of the political and economic system in Poland (including the discussions of the so-called Round Table), the representatives of farmers belonged to a group of enthusiastic advocates of a radical reduction of the role of the state in the economy, the establishment of conditions for the free influence of market mechanisms, and freedom in the social and economic activities of farmers. These postulates were implemented. The price of freedom proved, however, to be too high, especially for farmers. They bear the accumulated costs of the ineffectiveness of the past socialist system, probably to a greater degree than other social and economic groups. Since the Polish economy remains, to a large extent, a closed economy, farmers are forced to buy production inputs from the monopolistic domestic producers, who incorporate their low efficiency in the cost of production. Prices often exceed international prices. The shape of the structure of the food economy will not change as rapidly as did legal and political structures. The backward structure of peasant farms in Poland also does not favor increased productivity, as the average farm area is small and the fields are fragmented. Costs of production on such farms must be high.

The largest private sector that survived the period of communist rule in Central and Eastern Europe—that is, private family farms—has found itself in an economic situation more difficult than in the previous hostile and alien environment of the planned economy. The sought-after political and economic freedom proved in many respects a bitter experience that has resulted in the pains of the adjustment period. Almost all farmers agree that this process of adjustment must be rapidly concluded.

Bibliography

"Amendment to the Polish Foreign Exchange Law." *Dziennik Ustaw* 75 (1989): Item 441.

Bakcsi, Ildiko. "A Vallalattal Egyutt Vallalkozo Munkakozossegek" (Working Groups in Entrepreneurship with the Company). Unpublished manuscript, 1987.

Barzel, Yoram. *Economic Analysis of Property Rights*. Cambridge: Cambridge University Press, 1990.

Berent, T. Ivan and Gyorgy Ranki. *A Magyar Gazdasag Szaz Eve* (Hundred Years of the Hungarian Economy). Budapest: Kossuth Konyvkiado es Kozgazdasagi es Jogi Konyvkiado, 1972.

Berki, Sandor. *A Pesti Berkoczi* (The Taxis of Pest). Budapest: Institute of Sociology, 1990.

Binswanger, Hans. "The Policy Response of Agriculture." *Proceedings of the World Bank Annual Conference on Development Economics* (1989): 231–58.

Boffito, C. *Reforms and Export Promotion*. Torino, Italy: G. Einardi, 1988.

Bornstein, M. (ed.). *Comparative Economic Systems: Models and Cases*, 4th edn. Homewood, Ill.: Richard D. Irwin, 1979a.

_____. "Economic Reform in Eastern Europe." In *Comparative Economic Systems: Models and Cases*, 4th edn. M. Bornstein, ed. Homewood, Ill.: Richard D. Irwin, 1979b.

Brada, Josef C., Arthur E. King, and Dow E. Schlagenhauf. "Policymaking and Plan Construction in the Czechoslovak Fifth and Sixth Five-Year Plans." *East European Economic Assessment, Part I—Country Studies*. Washington, D.C.: Government Printing Office, 1981.

Brenner, Reuven. "The Eastern Block: Legal Reforms First, Monetary and Macroeconomic Policies Second." *Exchange Policies in Socialist*

Countries. San Francisco: International Center for Economic Growth, 1990.

Brus, Wlodzimierz. "The Political Economy of Reforms." In *Creditworthiness and Reform in Poland, Western and Polish Perspectives*. P. Marer and W. Siwinski, eds. Bloomington, Ind.: Indiana University Press, 1988.

Buchanan, David. "G24 Agrees Aid for East Europeans." *Financial Times* (December 6, 1990): 2.

Bulir, Ales. "Prispevek k Vymezeni Peneznich Pricin Inflace" (An Attempt at Determining the Monetary Causes of Inflation). *Politicka Ekonomie* 38 (7) (1990): 803–18.

Central Statistical Office. Warsaw, 1990.

Clarke, Roger A. (ed.). *Poland: The Economy in the 1980s*. Essex: Longman, 1989.

Csikos-Nagy, Bela. "The Hungarian Economic Reform After Ten Years." *Soviet Studies* 30 (4) (October 1978): 540–46.

"Enter Comrade Capitalist." *The Economist* 312 (7617): 36.

Esterhazy, Peter. *Termelesi-regeny* (Production Novel). Budapest: Magveto Kiado, 1979.

Federal Ministry of Social Affairs, Czechoslovak Federal Socialist Republic.

Feige, Edgar L. "Perestroika and Socialist Privatization: What is to be Done? And How?" *Comparative Economic Studies* 32 (3) (Fall 1990): 71–81.

Fischer, S. and W. Easterly. "The Economics of the Government Budget Constraint." *The World Bank Observer* 5 (2) (July 1990): 127–42.

Foreign Trade Research Institute. *Polish Foreign Trade in 1990. Annual Report* Warsaw: Foreign Trade Research Institute, 1990.

Gabor, R. Istvan and Tamas D. Horvath. "Bukas es Visszavoonulas a Magan Kisiparban" (Failure and Retreat in Private Small-scale Industry). *Kozgazdasago Szemle* 34 (4) (1987): 404–19.

Galbraith, John Kenneth. "Which Capitalism for Eastern Europe?" *Harper's Magazine* 280 (April 1990): 19–21.

Garfinkel, Michelle R. "What is an 'Acceptable' Rate of Inflation? A Review of the Issues." *Federal Reserve Bank of St. Louis Review* 71 (4) (1989): 3–15.

Garvy, George. *Money, Banking, and Credit in Eastern Europe*. New York: Federal Reserve Bank, 1966.

"The Gift of Capitalism." *The Economist* 316 (7664) (July 21, 1990): 13–14.

Goodhart, Charles. *Money, Information, and Uncertainty*. London: Macmillan Education, 1989.

Gorlach, Krzysztof. "On Repressive Tolerance: State and Peasant Farm in Poland." *Sociologia Ruralis* 29 (1) (1989): 23–33.

Granick, David. *Enterprise in Eastern Europe*. Princeton, N.J.: Princeton University Press, 1975.

Gregory, Paul and Robert Stuart. *Comparative Economic Systems*. Boston: Houghton-Mifflin, 1989.

Hafer, R. W. "Does Dollar Depreciation Cause Inflation?" *Federal Reserve Bank of St. Louis Review* 71 (4) (1989): 16–28.

Hajnoczy, Arpad. "Kie Lesz az UKO?" (To Whom Will OKU Belong? Artificial Intervention). *Figyelo* (March 29, 1990): 5.

Hamori, Balazs. *A Szocializmus Gaxdasagi Elmelete* (Economic Theory of Socialism). Budapest: Kozgazdasagi es Jogi-Konyvkiado, 1986.

Hansen, A. *Monetary Theory and Fiscal Policy.* New York: McGraw-Hill, 1949.

Havlik, Peter. "A Comparison of Purchasing Power Parity and Consumption Levels in Austria and Czechoslovakia." *Journal of Comparative Economics* 9 (2) (1985): 178–90.

Hewett, Edward A. "The Hungarian Economy: Lessons of the 1970s and Prospects for the 1980s." *U.S. Congress Committee, East European Economic Assessment, Part I.* Washington, D.C.: Government Printing Office, 1981.

Ickes, Barry W. "A Macroeconomic Model for Centrally Planned Economies." *Journal of Macroeconomics* 12 (Winter 1990): 23–46.

"Informacja Statystyczna o Sytuacji Spoleczno-Gospodarczej Kraju 1990" (Statistical Information on the Socio-Economic Situation of Poland 1990, Parts 1 and 2). Warsaw: Polish Central Statistical Office, 1990.

International Monetary Fund. *IMF Survey* 19 (4) (February 19, 1990).

Juhász, Pál. "Gondolatok a Gazdasági Reform Intézményi Megalapozásáról" (Ideas About the Institutional Foundation of the Economic Reform). *Medvetanc* 2 (1987).

Kaleta, József. *Droga do Rynku* (The Road to the Market). Warsaw: SWL, 1990.

Karsai, Gábor. "Kelet-Közép-Európa Különleges Esélye" (Particular Change of Central-Eastern Europe). Interview with Terez Laky. *Figyelo* (December 6, 1990): 11.

Kisszervezetek a Gazdaságban 1989, 1990 (Role of Small Organizations in the Economy 1989, 1990, Quarters 1–3). Budapest: Hungarian Central Statistical Office, December 1990.

Klacek, J. et al. *Macroeconomic Analysis.* Prague: National Institute of Economics, 1990.

Klaus, Vaclav. "Economic Disequilibrium and its Significance for Econometric Modelling: Some Comments." *Ekonomicko-matematicky Obzor* 25 (1) (1989): 19–34.

———. "Policy Dilemmas of Eastern European Reforms: Notes of an Insider." *Federal Reserve Bank of Kansas City Economic Review* 75 (5) (1990): 5–8.

Klekner, Peter. "Sok Vallalat—Keves Toke" (Many Companies—Little Capital). *Figyelo* (September 20, 1990).

Kornai, Janos. *Overcentralization in Economic Administration.* London: Oxford University Press, 1959.

———. *Anti-Equilibrium: On Economic Systems Theory and the Tasks of Research.* Amsterdam: North-Holland, 1971.

_____. *The Economics of Shortage.* Amsterdam: North Holland, 1980.

_____. *The Road to a Free Economy. Shifting from A Socialist System. The Example of Hungary.* New York: W. W. Norton, 1990.

Krueger, Anne O. "The Importance of Economic Policy in Development: Contrasts between Korea and Turkey." In *Protection and Competition in International Trade, Essays in Honor of W. M. Corden.* H. Kierzkowski, ed. Oxford: Basil Blackwell, 1987.

Kuczi, Tibor and Agnes Vajda. "A Kisvállalkozók Társadalmi Összetétele" (Social Composition of the Small Entrepreneurs). *Közgazdasági Szemle* 1 (1991).

Legget, Robert E. "Measuring Inflation in the Soviet Machine Building Sector, 1960–1973." *Journal of Comparative Economics* 5 (2) (1981): 169–84.

Lonc, Tomasz, Anna Szemberg, and Augustyn Woś. *Rural Development in Postwar Poland.* Stockholm: Stockholm School of Economics, 1989.

Marer, Paul. *Dollar GNPs and Growth Rates of USSR and Eastern Europe.* Baltimore: Johns Hopkins University Press, 1985.

Marer, Paul and W. Siwiński (eds.). *Creditworthiness and Reform in Poland, Western and Polish Perspective.* Bloomington, Ind.: Indiana University Press, 1988.

Marrese, Michael. "Perestroika and Socialist Privatization: A Comment." *Comparative Economic Studies* 32 (3) (Fall 1990): 55–61.

Mejstrik, Michal. "Where We Are Headed: The Case of Czechoslovakia." *German Reunification and the Privatization of Czechoslovakia, Hungary, and Poland: Implications for Western Business.* New York: New York University Press, 1991.

Millar, James R. "Perestroika and Socialist Privatization: What Is To Be Done? A Comment: There Is No Quick Fix." *Comparative Economic Studies* 32 (3) (Fall 1990): 62–70.

Montias, John M. *The Structure of Economic Systems.* New Haven: Yale University Press, 1976.

Neumann, László. *End of the Company Economic Work Group.* Budapest: Labour Research Institute, 1989.

_____. "Egy Privatizálási Alternativa: Nagy Ipari Szervezetekból Kiváló Magánvállalkozások" (An Alternative of Privatization: Private Entrepreneurship Leaving the Huge Industrial Organizations). *Közgazdasági Szemle* 6 (1990).

Nuti, D. M. "The Pace of Change in Central and Eastern Europe." *Mocm-Most* 1 (1991): 3.

Piotrowski, J. *Poland's Foreign Trade Regime in 1990.* Foreign Trade Research Institute Discussion Paper II. Warsaw: Foreign Trade Research Institute, 1990.

Pitzner-Joergensen, F. "Economic Reform and East-West Trade and Cooperation." Verona, Italy: University of Verona, 1990.

"Polish Customs Duty Law." *Journal of Laws* 75 (1989): Item 445.

Portes, Richard and David Winter. "The Demand for Money and for Consumption Goods in Centrally Planned Economies." *The Review of Economics and Statistics* 60 (1) (1978): 8–18.

Pukli, Péter. *A Kisvállakoz Helyzete, Müködési Feltételei, További Fejlódési Lehetóségei Magyarországon* (The Small Ventures: Place, Working Conditions, Further Possibilities of Development in Hungary). Budapest: Hungarian Central Statistical Office, 1990.

Ribnikar, Ivan. "Money and Finance in Yugoslavia," *Slovene Studies* 11(1–2) (1989): 57–64.

Robinson, William F. *The Pattern of Reform in Hungary: A Political, Economic, and Cultural Analysis*. New York: Praeger, 1973.

Rosen, Corey, Katherine J. Klein, and Karen Young. *Employee Ownership in America: The Equity Solution*. Lexington, Mass.: Lexington Books, 1985.

"Ruling by the Polish Minister for Foreign Economic Relations." *Dziennik Ustaw* 73 (1989): Item 432.

Sargent, Thomas J. "The Ends of Four Big Inflations." *Inflation: Causes and Effects*. Chicago: University of Chicago Press, 1982.

Slabek, Henryk. "Reforma Rolna" (Agrarian Reform). *Gospodarka Polski Ludowej 1944–1945*. Warsaw: KiW Publishers, 1978.

Slay, B. "Foreign Trade Reforms since 1981." In *Creditworthiness and Reform in Poland, Western and Polish Perspective*. P. Marer and W. Siwiński, eds. Bloomington, Ind.: Indiana Free Press, 1988.

Stark, David. "Vegyesgazdaság a Szocialista Vállalaton Belül" (Mixed Economy within the Socialist Firm). *Közgazdasági Szemle* 35 (5) (1988): 584–602.

Swine, Nigel. *Collective Farms Which Work*. Cambridge: Oxford University Press, 1985.

Szabó, Jenó and Péter Csicsák. "Munkahelyteremtés és Kisvállalkozás." *Munkaügyi Szemle* 34 (4) (1990).

Szcxepański, Jan. "Rola Chlopów w Rozwoju Spoleczeństwa Polskiego" (The Role of Peasants in the Development of the Polish Society). *Odmiany Czasu Teraźniejszego*. Warsaw: KiW Publishers, 1975.

Szelényi, Iván. "Polgárosodás Magyarországon" (Development of Bourgeois Mentality in Hungary). *Valóság* 1 (1990).

Szelényi, Iván and Róbert Manchin. "Megszakított Polgárosodás" (Interrupted Development of Bourgeois Mentality). *Szociológia* 2 (1988): 121–52.

Tardos, Marton. "Options in Hungary's Foreign Trade." *Acta Oeconomica* 26 (1–2) (1981): 29–49.

Vickers, John. *Privatization: An Economic Analysis*. Cambridge, Mass.: MIT Press, 1988.

Wadekin, Karl-Eugen (ed.). *Communist Agriculture: Farming in the Soviet Union and Eastern Europe*. London: Routledge, 1990.

Wapenhans, Willi. "Les Reformes Economiques Dans les Pays d'Europe de l'Est: Une Gageure" (The Challenge of Economic Reforms in East Europe). *Finances et Developpement* 27 (4) (December 1990): 2–5.

Wiles, Peter J. D. *Economic Institutions Compared.* Oxford: Basil Blackwell, 1979.

Wilkin, Jerzy. "Przemiany w Rolnictwie a Teoria Gospodarki Socjalistycznej" (Transformations in Agriculture and the Theory of the Socialist Economy). *Wieś i Rolnictwo* 2 (1986).

————. "The Induced Innovation Model of Agricultural Development and the Socialist Economic System." *European Review of Agriculture Economics* 15 (2–3) (1988): 211–20.

Williamson, Oliver E. *Economic Institutions of Capitalism.* New York: The Free Press, 1985.

World Bank Staff. *Poland—Reform, Adjustment and Growth.* Washington, D.C.: World Bank, 1987.

Zieleniec, Jozef. "Microeconomic Categories in Different Economic Systems: The Firm." In *Optimal Decisions in Markets and Planned Economies.* Richard E. Quandt and Dusan Triska, eds. Boulder, Colo.: Westview Press, 1990.

Index

About the Contributors

ZOLTAN BARA is on the faculty of the Department of Economics at Budapest University of Economics in Hungary.

ALES BULIR is on the faculty of the Department of Monetary Theory and Policy at the Prague School of Economics in Czechoslovakia.

JIRI HLAVACEK is on the faculty of the Institute of Economics at Charles University in Czechoslovakia.

MACIEJ IWANEK is on the faculty of the Department of Economics at the University of Warsaw in Poland.

BERNARD S. KATZ is on the faculty of the Department of Economics and Business at Lafayette College in Pennsylvania.

ANDREJ KONDRATOWICZ is on the faculty of the Department of Economics at the University of Warsaw.

JAN MICHALEK is on the faculty of the Department of Economics at the University of Warsaw.

IVAN RIBNIKAR is on the faculty of the Department of Economics at the University of Ljubljana in Yugoslavia.

LIBBY RITTENBERG is on the faculty of the Department of Economics and Business at Colorado College.

JERZY SKURATOWICZ is on the faculty of the Department of Economics at the University of Warsaw.

MIECZYSLAW W. SOCHA is on the faculty of the Department of Economics at the University of Warsaw.

MILAN SOJKA is on the faculty of the Institute of Economics at Charles University.

KATALIN SZABO is on the faculty of the Department of Economics at Budapest University of Economics.

URSZULA SZTANDERSKA is on the faculty of the Department of Economics at the University of Warsaw.

JERZY WILKIN is on the faculty of the Department of Economics at the University of Warsaw.